LOVE · MARRIAGE · LOSS · JOURNEYS

MARRIAGE

Also in this series

CHILDHOOD
Edited by Kate Figes

FIRST LOVE
Edited by Paul Bailey

FRIENDSHIP
Edited by Shena Mackay

JOURNEYS
Edited by Charles Nicholl

LOSS
Edited by Elspeth Barker

MARRIAGE

EDITED BY

Elizabeth Jane Howard

J. M. Dent London

First published in Great Britain in 1997
by J. M. Dent

This selection and introduction © Elizabeth Jane Howard, 1997

The moral right of Elizabeth Jane Howard to be identified as the
Editor of this work has been asserted in accordance with the
Copyright, Designs and Patents Act of 1988.

A CIP catalogue record for this book is available
from the British Library

ISBN 0 460 87931 6

Typeset at The Spartan Press Ltd,
Lymington, Hants
Set in 10/11½ Photina
Printed in Great Britain by
Clays Ltd, St Ives plc

J. M. Dent

Weidenfeld & Nicolson
The Orion Publishing Group Ltd
Orion House
5 Upper Saint Martin's Lane
London, WC2H 9EA

CONTENTS

❧

Part Two: Loss

Part Three: The Wear and Tear of Married Life

Part Four: The Rough

Part Five: The Best of It

INTRODUCTION

A pragmatic, often unnervingly acquisitive attitude to marriage has been resolutely inherent since the institution was founded. Marriage was not only to ensure blood lines of families, it was useful, sometimes necessary, for acquiring more land, for patching up feuds with neighbours, for becoming more powerful and so on. Some, if not all of these notions persisted right through to the beginning of this century, for, up until then, marriage was the only respectable career for young gentlewomen. The alternative of being a governess did not commonly lead to blind owners of large houses – with first (mad) wives conveniently burned to death – professing undying love. We even have the intensely romantic Marianne Dashwood's ruminations on the subject that show a degree of practicality uncharacteristic of her. So many girls were sold or coerced or simply escaped into marriage; and if it proved to be an unhappy trap there was no way out: a wife with children and utterly dependent upon her husband had no choice but to stay with him. Marriage was also a way of making sex respectable and was therefore upheld by all major religions.

But with all of these social and emotional pressures, the idea and the ideal of marriage has been recognised and practised in its purest form. There have always been men and women who have fallen in love, have risked everything to commit themselves to each other, have brought up their children and ended their lives in a companionship that is unique in its depth and completeness. It is infinitely more interesting to have different experiences with the same person rather than to repeat the same experiences with different people; and really to know and love another person and to be known and loved by them is the most rewarding experience we can have with each other. It is well worth exercising the utmost discrimination (choosing a partner who is equally committed), self-knowledge and patience (the things that irritate one most about other people are usually also one's own shortcomings), and *kindness* – not associated with love often enough in my view, but who does not respond to it?

PART ONE

Proposals – Arrangements

INTRODUCTION

This part is all to do with the beginnings of marriage: proposals, asseverations, and accounts and results of arrangements made by interested parties; for instance, heirs to thrones being paired off with healthy, amenable girls who sometimes confounded their mothers-in-law or family with the unexpected sincerity of their love. What is fascinating is trying to see whether the success or failure of the subsequent marriages is endemic: in the case of fiction this is sometimes difficult because many novels end with their protagonists becoming engaged, although since Daisy Ashford, the author of our second piece, was nine when she wrote her novel, living happily ever after would, I think, have been seriously expected. Queen Victoria had to do the proposing as she was already Queen when her Uncle Leopold sent the Saxe-Coburg brothers over for her inspection. She fell in love with Albert on sight and, apart from how he felt about her, his remarkable sense of duty was some insurance of her happiness. The Princess May was, like the Spanish princess Catherine of Aragon, destined to marry an older brother, who in both cases died, whereupon they were handed on to the next heir to the throne, Henry VIII and George V respectively. Queen Mary also had a profound sense of duty to the monarchy, but this seems to have helped rather than hindered her natural feeling for her husband. Catherine the Great had to find *two* wives for her son Paul as the first one died after three years of marriage. The seventeen-year-old Sophie Dorothea of Württemberg can have had no idea of what she was taking on when she married Paul, who, apart from being a tyrannical autocrat, was unstable to the point of madness. Chekhov's letters to the actress whom he loved and married are so beguiling that it must almost have been worth being apart in order to receive them.

This is in stark contrast to the deliberations of Saint-Simon at the court of Louis XIV and the even chillier inspection by the bridegroom of Teresa Ghiselli who became Byron's last attachment. Finally, there is the lyrical tale of 'The Owl and the Pussy-Cat', which shows that one should never be afraid of attaching oneself to someone apparently very different. I am not sure that, apart from a mutual interest in mice, they had much else in common.

MICHEL DE MONTAIGNE

♥

from *Essays*

A good marriage, if such there be, rejects the company and conditions of love. It tries to reproduce those of friendship. It is a sweet association in life, full of constancy, trust, and an infinite number of useful and solid services and mutual obligations. No woman who savours the taste of it ... would want to have the place of a mistress or paramour to her husband. If she is lodged in his affection as a wife, she is lodged there much more honourably and securely. When he dances ardent and eager attention elsewhere, still let anyone ask him then on whom he would rather have some shame fall, on his wife or his mistress; whose misfortune would afflict him more; for whom he wishes more honour. These question admit of no doubt in a sound marriage.

DAISY ASHFORD

❧

from *The Young Visiters*

The hero proposes to the heroine
She looked very beautifull with some red roses in her hat
and the dainty red ruge in her cheeks looked quite the thing.
Bernard heaved a sigh and his eyes flashed as he beheld her
and Ethel thorght to herself what a fine type of manhood he
reprisented . . .

Bernard sat beside her in profound silence gazing at her
pink face and long wavy eye lashes . . .

Ethel he murmured in a trembly voice.

Oh what is it said Ethel hastily sitting up.

Word fail me ejaculated Bernard horsly my passion for
you is intense he added fervently. It has grown day and
night since I first beheld you.

Oh said Ethel in supprise I am not prepared for this and
she lent back against the trunk of the tree.

Bernard placed one arm tightly round her. When will you
marry me Ethel he uttered you must be my wife it has come
to that I love you so intensly that if you say no I shall
perforce dash my body to the brink of yon muddy river he
panted wildly.

Oh dont do that implored Ethel breathing rarther hard.

Then say you love me he cried.

Oh Bernard she sighed fervently I certainly love you

madly you are to me like a Heathen god she cried looking at his manly form and handsome flashing face I will indeed marry you.

QUEEN VICTORIA

❦

Proposal and Honeymoon

Next morning, about half past twelve, the Prince was summoned to a private audience. 'I said to him', wrote the Queen, 'that I thought he must be aware *why* I wished them to come here, and that it would make me *too happy* if he would consent to what I wished (to marry me); we embraced each other over and over again, and he was *so* kind, *so* affectionate; Oh! to *feel* I was, and am, loved by *such* an Angel as Albert was *too great delight to describe*! he is *perfection*; perfection in every way – in beauty – in everything! I told him I was quite unworthy of him and kissed his dear hand – he said he would be very happy "das Leben mit dir zu zubringen" [to share life with you] and was so kind and seemed so happy, that I really felt it was the happiest brightest moment in my life, which made up for all I had suffered and endured. Oh! *how* I adore and love him, I cannot say!! *how* I will strive to make him feel as little as possible the great sacrifice he has made; I told him it was a great sacrifice – which he wouldn't allow . . . I feel the happiest of human beings.

'He [Prince Albert] was *so* affectionate, *so* kind, *so* dear. We kissed each other again and again and he called me [in German] "Darling little one, I love you *so* much" and that we should have a very fortunate life together. Oh! what *too* sweet delightful moments are these!! Oh! how *blessed*, how happy I am to think he is *really* mine; I can scarcely believe myself *so blessed*. I kissed his dear hand and so feel *so* grateful to him; he is such an Angel, such a *very* great Angel! We sit so nicely side by side on that little blue sofa; no two Lovers could ever be happier than we are! . . . He took my hands in his, and said my hands were so little he could hardly believe they *were* hands, as he had hitherto *only* been accustomed to handle hands like Ernest's.'

Here is the first night of the honeymoon
When the Queen had looked over the rooms she and the Prince were to occupy and changed her dress, she joined the Prince in his room; he was playing the piano and had changed into his Windsor coat. He took the Queen in his arms and kissed and caressed her, and 'was so dear and kind. We had our dinner in our sitting-room, but I had such a sick headache that I could eat nothing, and was obliged to lie down . . . for the remainder of the evening on the sofa; but ill or not, I *never, never* spent such an evening!! My *dearest dearest dear* Albert sat on a footstool by my side, and his excessive love and affection gave me feelings of heavenly love and happiness I never could have *hoped* to have felt before! He clasped me in his arms, and we kissed each other again and again! His beauty, his sweetness and gentleness – really how can I ever be thankful enough to have such a *Husband*! . . . to be called by names of tenderness, I have never yet heard used to me before – was bliss beyond belief! Oh! this was the happiest day of my life! May God help me to do my duty as I ought and be worthy of such blessings!'

Next day to have the Prince's 'beautiful angelic face' to greet her in the morning was more joy than the Queen could express. They got up at half past eight, much earlier than the Queen's usual hour, and Greville, still grumpy, told Lady Palmerston that the wedding night had been too short, that this was 'not the way to provide us with a Prince of Wales'. Albert breakfasted in a black velvet jacket without any neckcloth so that his throat could be seen 'and looked more beautiful,' wrote the Queen, 'than it is possible for me to say.' They then walked on the Terrace and New Walk, alone arm in arm. It was now the turn of the Prince to feel sick, as he had not yet recovered from the effects of his seasickness followed by the festivities and banquets attendant on the marriage in addition to the strain of the ceremony itself. He lay down and dozed in the Queen's sitting-room while she wrote letters, getting up at one point to read her a funny story but feeling so poorly that he was forced to lie down again, resting his head on her shoulder. That evening, the second of the honeymoon, was not spent alone with the Queen. There were ten people at dinner, a 'very delightful merry, nice little party', wrote the Queen. Prince Albert recovered sufficiently to be able to sing, though he still felt weak in his knees.

❥

from *The Importance of Being Earnest*

JACK Charming day it has been, Miss Fairfax.

GWENDOLEN Pray don't talk to me about the weather, Mr Worthing. Whenever people talk to me about the weather, I always feel quite certain that they mean something else. And that makes me so nervous.

JACK I do mean something else.

GWENDOLEN I thought so. In fact, I am never wrong.

JACK And I would like to be allowed to take advantage of Lady Bracknell's temporary absence . . .

GWENDOLEN I would certainly advise you to do so. Mamma has a way of coming back suddenly into a room that I have often had to speak to her about.

JACK (*nervously*) Miss Fairfax, ever since I met you I have admired you more than any girl . . . I have ever met since . . . I met you.

GWENDOLEN Yes, I am quite well aware of the fact. And I often wish that in public, at any rate, you had been more demonstrative. For me you have always had an irresistible fascination. Even before I met you I was far from indifferent to you. (JACK *looks at her in amazement*) We live, as I hope you know, Mr Worthing, in an age of ideals. The fact is constantly mentioned in the more expensive monthly magazines, and has reached the provincial pulpits, I am told; and my ideal has always been to love someone of the name of Ernest. There is something in that name that inspires absolute confidence. The moment Algernon first mentioned to me that he had a friend called Ernest, I knew I was destined to love you.

JACK You really love me, Gwendolen?

GWENDOLEN Passionately!

JACK Darling! You don't know how happy you've made me.

GWENDOLEN My own Ernest!

JACK But you don't really mean to say that you couldn't love me if my name wasn't Ernest?

GWENDOLEN But your name is Ernest.

JACK Yes, I know it is. But supposing it was something else? Do you mean to say you couldn't love me then?

GWENDOLEN (*glibly*) Ah! that is clearly a metaphysical speculation, and like most metaphysical speculation has very little reference at all to the actual facts of real life, as we know them.

JACK Personally, darling, to speak quite candidly, I don't much care about the name of Ernest . . . I don't think the name suits me at all.

GWENDOLEN It suits you perfectly. It is a divine name. It has a music of its own. It produces vibrations.

JACK Well, really, Gwendolen, I must say that I think there are lots of other much nicer names. I think Jack, for instance, a charming name.

GWENDOLEN Jack? . . . No, there is very little music in the name Jack, if any at all, indeed. It does not thrill. It produces absolutely no vibrations . . . I have known several Jacks, and they all, without exception, were more than usually plain. Besides, Jack is a notorious domesticity for John! And I pity any woman who is married to a man called John. She would probably never be allowed to know the entrancing pleasure of a single moment's solitude. The only really safe name is Ernest.

JACK Gwendolen, I must get christened at once – I mean we must get married at once. There is no time to be lost.

GWENDOLEN Married, Mr Worthing?

JACK (*astounded*) Well . . . surely. You know that I love you, and you led me to believe, Miss Fairfax, that you were not absolutely indifferent to me.

GWENDOLEN I adore you. But you haven't proposed to me yet. Nothing has been said at all about marriage. The subject has not even been touched on.

JACK Well . . . may I propose to you now?

GWENDOLEN I think it would be an admirable opportunity. And to spare you any possible disappointment, Mr Worthing, I think it only fair to tell you quite frankly beforehand that I am fully determined to accept you.

JACK Gwendolen!

GWENDOLEN Yes, Mr Worthing, what have you got to say to me?

JACK You know what I have got to say to you.

GWENDOLEN Yes, but you don't say it.

JACK Gwendolen, will you marry me?

(*Goes on his knees*)

GWENDOLEN Of course I will, darling. How long you have been about it! I am afraid you have had very little experience in how to propose.

JACK My own one, I have never loved anyone in the world but you.

GWENDOLEN Yes, but men often propose for practice. I know my brother Gerald does. All my girl friends tell me so. What wonderfully blue eyes you have, Ernest! They are quite, quite, blue. I hope you will always look at me just like that, especially when there are other people present.

THOMAS HARDY

from *Jude the Obscure*

He knew well, too well, in the secret centre of his brain, that Arabella was not worth a great deal as a specimen of womankind. Yet, such being the custom of the rural districts among honourable young men who had drifted so far into intimacy with a woman as he unfortunately had done, he was ready to abide by what he had said, and take the consequences. For his own soothing he kept up a factitious belief in her. His idea of her was the thing of most consequence, not Arabella herself, he sometimes said laconically.

The banns were put in and published the very next Sunday. The people of the parish all said what a simple fool young Fawley was. All his reading had only come to this, that he would have to sell his books to buy saucepans. Those who guessed the probable state of affairs, Arabella's parents being among them, declared that it was the sort of conduct they would have expected of such an honest young man as Jude in reparation of the wrong he had done his innocent sweetheart. The parson who married them seemed to think it satisfactory too.

And so, standing before the aforesaid officiator, the two swore that at every other time of their lives till death took them, they would assuredly believe, feel, and desire precisely as they had believed, felt, and desired during the few preceding weeks. What was as remarkable as the undertaking itself was the fact that nobody seemed at all surprised at what they swore.

ANTON CHEKHOV

Letters to Olga Knipper

Yalta, Thursday, 26 April 1901

Dog Olga! I shall come early in May. As soon as you get my telegram, go immediately to the Dresden hotel and inquire if Room 45 is free, in other words, reserve a cheap room.

I often see Nemirovich, he is very nice, does not put on airs; I haven't yet seen his spouse. I am coming to Moscow chiefly to gallivant and gorge myself. We'll go to Petrovsko-Razumovskoe, to Zvenigorod – we'll go everywhere, provided the weather is good. If you consent to go down the Volga with me, we'll eat sturgeon.

Kuprin is apparently in love – under an enchantment. He fell in love with a huge, husky woman whom you know and whom you advised me to marry.

If you give me your word that not a soul in Moscow will know about our wedding until it has taken place, I am ready to marry you on the very day of my arrival. For some reason I am terribly afraid of the wedding ceremony and congratulations and the champagne that you must hold in your hand while you smile vaguely. I wish we could go straight from church to Zvenigorod. Or perhaps we could get married in Zvenigorod. Think, think, darling! You are clever, they say.

The weather in Yalta is rather wretched. A fierce wind. The roses are blooming, but not fully; they will, though. The irises are magnificent.

Everything is all right with me, except for one trifle: my health.

Gorky has not been deported, but arrested; he is held in Nizhny. Posse, too, has been arrested.

I embrace you, Olga.

Your Antoine

In a letter of 23 December Olga writes: 'It is such torture for me to think that I can't be beside you, to tend you, change compresses, feed you, comfort you. I imagine how you suffered. I give my word that this is the last such year, my own. I'll do everything to make your life pleasant, warm, no longer lonely, and you'll see, you will be happy with me and you will write, work. In your heart you probably reproach me for not loving you enough. Isn't it true? You reproach me for not chucking the theatre, not being a wife to you.'

Yalta, 29 December 1901

You are foolish, darling. Never once since I have been married did I reproach you about the theatre; on the contrary, I have rejoiced that you are at work, that you have a purpose in life, that you are not aimlessly dangling like your husband. I don't write you about my illness because I am already well. My temperature is normal, I eat five eggs a day, drink milk, and then there is dinner which, since Masha is here, is delicious. Do your work, darling, don't bustle about, above all, do not yield to depression.

Well, my little slattern, good-bye, keep well! Don't dare to mope, don't lament. Laugh! I embrace you and regret that this is all.

There was no letter from you yesterday. What a lazy-bones you have become! Ah, dog that you are, you dog!

Well, darling, my good, lovely wife, I kiss you warmly and hug you again warmly. I think of you very often, you too think of me.

Your Ant.

Yalta, 20 January 1902

How foolish you are, my darling, what a silly! Why are you sulking? What about? You write that everything about your career is exaggerated and that you are a complete nonentity: that I'm tired of your letters, that you are horrified to feel your life narrowing, and so on, and so on. What a silly you are! I didn't write you about my future play not because I have no faith in you, as you write, but because as yet I have no faith in the play. It is just beginning to glimmer in my brain like the earliest ray of dawn, and I myself don't yet know what it is like, what will come of it, and it keeps changing from day to day. If we were face to face, I would talk to you about it, but I mustn't write about it, because I wouldn't be able to put anything down on paper, but would only scribble nonsense and then grow cold to the subject. In your letter you threaten never to ask me about anything, never to meddle in anything; but why do you treat me so, my darling? No, you are a kind soul, wrath will give place to mercy when once more you see how much I love you, how close you are to me, how I can't live without you, my little silly. Give up moping, give it up! Burst out laughing! I am permitted to mope, for I live in a desert, have nothing to do, see no one and am ill every week but you? Somehow your life is full . . .

By the way, Gorky is preparing to start work on a new play about the life of people in a flophouse, though I advise him to wait a year or two, not to be in a hurry. A writer must write a good deal, but he ought not hurry. Isn't that so, my spouse?

On 17 January, my name day, I was in a disgusting mood, because I felt ill and because the telephone kept clamouring, bringing me telegrams of congratulation. Even you and Masha didn't spare me.

Incidentally, when is your *Geburtstag*?

You write: don't be sad – we shall soon see each other. What does this mean? Do we meet in Holy Week? Or sooner? Don't upset me, my joy. In December you wrote me that you would come in January, you disturbed me, you stirred me up; then you began writing that you were coming in Holy Week – and I commanded my soul to be still, I hemmed myself in, and now again you are suddenly raising a storm on the Black Sea. What for? . . .

And so, my wife, nice, good, golden one, may God protect you, be well and cheerful, think of your husband at least in the evening, at bedtime. Above all, don't be dejected. You know your husband is not a drunkard, not a spendthrift, not a ruffian; in my behaviour I am totally a German husband; I even wear warm drawers . . .

I embrace my wife one hundred and one times and kiss her endlessly.

Your Ant.

You write, 'No matter where I turn – walls everywhere.' And where did you turn?

Yalta, 20 September 1902

Olga, my sweet little muzzle, greetings! Your latest letters showed you sunk in melancholy, and perhaps already turned into a nun, while I am so eager to see you! I shall come soon, soon, and, I repeat, stay until you chase me out, even till January. Mother leaves Yalta on 3 October – at

18

least that's what she said yesterday. First she will go to Petersburg and then, returning from there, will stay in Moscow with Ivan. That's my advice to her.

Why are you so troubled about my share in the corporation financing the Art Theatre under the direction of Morozov? It doesn't matter. When I reach Moscow I'll talk to him about it, but in the meantime, leave him alone, darling.

And so I shall go to Moscow without a spittoon, and in a railway car, oh, what a nuisance it is. Don't send it, the package may come too late. Order Masha to fry a veal croquette, the kind that costs 30 copecks. And get Stritzky's 'Export' beer. By the way, nowadays I eat a great deal, but I find that I still have little strength and energy and I have been coughing again, and once more started drinking Ems water. But my mood is not bad, I don't notice how the day passes. Well, these are all trifles.

You are right that if we were to continue to live together I should grow tired of you, for I would get used to you as to a table, a chair. 'You and I, both of us, are somehow unfinished creatures.' I don't know, darling, whether I am finished or not, but I am certain that the longer we two live together, the broader and deeper my love for you will become. Make a note of this, little actress. If it weren't for my illness, it would be hard to find a man more of a stay-at-home than I.

Day before yesterday there were a few drops of rain and yesterday during the day there were more, and that was all. The sun is as scorching as before, everything is dry. You should have a talk with Taube about your intestines. Has he returned from abroad? Did you inquire? You know, melancholy is caused by intestinal trouble, remember that. In old age, because of this ailment you will beat your husband and your children. Beat them, and at the same time sob.

19

Altschuller will come tomorrow, will auscultate me – for the first time this autumn. I kept putting him off but now it's rather awkward to do so. He kept scaring me and threatening to write to you. (Here in Yalta everyone thinks for some reason that you are a harsh one, and that you keep me under your thumb).

What else, then? Well, I kiss my little bug. Write me about your health in greater detail. I repeat: see Taube, and again, write. And so I kiss and stroke your back, and then embrace you. Good-bye.

Your A.

QUEEN MARY

Her Second Engagement

This sultry, oppressive weather lasted all through the eight weeks' engagement which ended with the wedding day, 6 July. As this climax drew nearer and nearer, the nerves of the young couple became more and more strung up. To begin with, the Duchess of Teck would never leave them alone together. Prince George complained of this to his fiancée, who replied that Princess Mary Adelaide was '*so obstinate . . .*'

The fact is [this sagacious letter continues] that we are all in a worried bustled state of mind & things irritate & annoy us which otherwise we should not bother about, I know I am always losing my temper with somebody or something & I assure you this is not generally the case, as I know only too well how much bad tempered people make one suffer. This is a simply *horrid* time we are going through & I am only looking forward to the time when you & I shall be alone at Sandringham . . . I am very sorry that I am still so shy with you, I tried not to be so the other day, but alas failed, I was angry with myself! It is so stupid to be so stiff together & really there is nothing I would not tell you, except that I *love* you more than anybody in the world, & this I cannot tell you myself so I write it to relieve my feelings.

To this letter Prince George replied the same day with a long, affectionate note, a part of which reads:

> ... Thank God we both understand each other, & I think it really unnecessary for me to tell you how deep my love for you my darling is & I feel it growing stronger & stronger every time I see you; although I may appear shy & cold. But this worry & busy time is most annoying & when we do meet it is only [to] talk business ...

Engagements are well known to have nerve-racking moments; and we may think that this particular engagement, with all its antecedent sorrows and rumours, generated a pitch of nervous tension all its own. Also Princess Mary Adelaide drove her daughter hard during these weeks: 'Simply tell Aunt Mary that you won't do any more and that I don't wish it,' Prince George wrote on 12 June. 'I hope you are quite well again, I am nearly *dead*,' wrote Princess May some days later.

On the morning of the wedding day, 6 July 1893, Princess May sent Prince George a pencilled note from Buckingham Palace, where she and her mother were staying:

> I should like to give you a wedding ring if you will wear it for my sake – I therefore send you herewith one or two to try on for size – Let me have the one you choose at once & I will give it to you in the chapel. What a memorable day in our lives this will be. God grant it may bring us much happiness. I love you with all my heart. Yrs for ever & ever – May.

On the morning, before starting for the Chapel Royal, Prince George accidentally caught sight of his bride down the long, long vista of one of the red-carpeted corridors of Buckingham Palace. He swept her a low and courtly bow. This gesture she never forgot.

FRANZ KAFKA

❦

For and Against Marriage

21 July 1913

Summary of all the arguments for and against my marriage:

1. Inability to endure life alone, which does not imply inability to live, quite the contrary, it is even improbable that I know how to live with anyone, but I am incapable, alone, of bearing the assault of my own life, the demands of my own person, the attacks of time and old age, the vague pressure of the desire to write, sleeplessness, the nearness of insanity — I cannot bear all this alone. I naturally add a 'perhaps' to this. The connexion with F. will give my existence more strength to resist.

2. Everything immediately gives me pause. Every joke in the comic paper, what I remember about Flaubert and Grillparzer, the sight of the nightshirts on my parents' beds, laid out for the night, Max's marriage. Yesterday my sister said, 'All the married people (that we know) are happy, I don't understand it,' this remark too gave me pause, I became afraid again.

3. I must be alone a great deal. What I accomplished was only the result of being alone.

4. I hate everything that does not relate to literature, conversations bore me (even if they relate to literature), to

23

visit people bores me, the sorrows and joys of my relatives bore me to my soul. Conversations take the importance, the seriousness, the truth of everything I think.

5. The fear of the connexion, of passing into the other. Then I'll never be alone again.

6. In the past, especially, the person I am in the company of my sisters has been entirely different from the person I am in the company of other people. Fearless, powerful, surprising, moved as I otherwise am only when I write. If through the intermediation of my wife I could be like that in the presence of everyone! But then would it not be at the expense of my writing? Not that, not that!

7. Alone, I could perhaps some day really give up my job. Married, it will never be possible.

Kafka, though twice engaged to Felice Bauer in the period between 1912 and 1917, broke off the engagement each time and never married. He once wrote to her:

My health is only just good enough for myself alone, not good enough for marriage, let alone fatherhood.

WILLIAM CONGREVE

from *The Way of the World*

MILLAMANT It may be in things of common application, but never, sure, in love. Oh, I hate a lover that can dare to think he draws a moment's air independent on the bounty of his mistress. There is not so impudent a thing in nature as the saucy look of an assured man, confident of success. The pedantic arrogance of a very husband has not so pragmatical an air. Ah, I'll never marry unless I am first made sure of my will and pleasure.

MIRABELL Would you have 'em both before marriage? Or will you be contented with the first now, and stay for the other till after grace?

MILLAMANT Ah, don't be impertinent. My dear liberty, shall I leave thee? My faithful solitude, my darling contempla-tion, must I bid you then adieu? Ay-h, adieu. My morning thoughts, agreeable wakings, indolent slumbers, all ye *douceurs*, ye *sommeils du matin*, adieu. I can't do't; 'tis more than impossible. Positively, Mirabell, I'll lie abed in a morning as long as I please.

MIRABELL Then I'll get up in a morning as early as I please.

MILLAMANT Ah, idle creature, get up when you will. And, d'ye hear, I won't be called names after I'm married; positively, I won't be called names.

MIRABELL Names?

MILLAMANT Ay, as wife, spouse, my dear, joy, jewel, love, sweetheart, and the rest of that nauseous cant, in which men and their wives are so fulsomely familiar. I shall never bear that. Good Mirabell, don't let us be familiar or fond, nor kiss before folks, like my Lady Fadler and Sir Francis; nor go to Hyde Park together the first Sunday in a new chariot, to provoke eyes and whispers; and then never be seen there together again, as if we were proud of one another the first week and ashamed of one another ever after. Let us never visit together, nor go to a play together, but let us be very strange and well-bred. Let us be as strange as if we had been married a great while, and as well-bred as if we were not married at all.

MIRABELL Have you any more conditions to offer? Hitherto your demands are pretty reasonable.

MILLAMANT Trifles! – As liberty to pay and receive visits to and from whom I please, to write and receive letters, without interrogatories or wry faces on your part. To wear what I please, and choose conversation with regard only to my own taste. To have no obligation upon me to converse with wits that I don't like, because they are your acquaintance, or to be intimate with fools because they may be your relations. Come to dinner when I please, dine in my dressing-room when I'm out of humour, without giving a reason. To have my closet inviolate. To be sole empress of my tea-table, which you must never presume to approach without first asking leave. And lastly, wherever I am, you shall always knock at the door before you come in. These articles subscribed, if I continue to endure you a little longer, I may by degrees dwindle into a wife.

MIRABELL Your bill of fare is something advanced in this latter account. Well, have I liberty to offer conditions, that when you are dwindled into a wife, I may not be beyond measure enlarged into a husband?

MILLAMANT You have free leave. Propose your utmost; speak and spare not.

MIRABELL I thank you. *Imprimis* then: I covenant that your acquaintance be general; that you admit no sworn confidante or intimate of your own sex; no she-friend to screen her affairs under your countenance and tempt you to make trial of a mutual secrecy. No decoy-duck to wheedle you a fop, scrambling to the play in a mask; then bring you home in a pretended fright, when you think you shall be found out, and rail at me for missing the play, and disappointing the frolic which you had to pick me up and prove my constancy.

MILLAMANT Detestable *imprimis*! I go to the play in a mask!

MIRABELL *Item*: I article that you continue to like your own face as long as I shall; and while it passes current with me, that you endeavour not to new-coin it. To which end, together with all vizards for the day, I prohibit all masks for the night, made of oiled skins and I know not what – hog's bones, hare's gall, pig-water, and the marrow of a roasted cat. In short, I forbid all commerce with the gentlewoman in what-d'ye-call-it Court. *Item*: I shut my doors against all bawds with baskets and pennyworths of muslin, china, fans, atlasses, etc. *Item*: When you shall be breeding—

MILLAMANT Ah, name it not.

MIRABELL Which may be presumed, with a blessing on our endeavours—

MILLAMANT Odious endeavours!

MIRABELL I denounce against all strait-lacing, squeezing for a shape till you mould my boy's head like a sugar-loaf, and instead of a man-child, make me father to a crooked billet. Lastly, to the dominion of the tea-table I submit, but with proviso that you exceed not in your province, but restrain yourself to native and simple tea-table drinks, as tea, chocolate, and coffee. As likewise to genuine and authorised tea-table talk, such as mending of fashions, spoiling reputations, railing at absent friends, and so forth; but that on no account you encroach upon the men's prerogative, and presume to drink healths or toast fellows; for prevention of which, I banish all foreign forces, all auxiliaries to the tea-table, as orange brandy, all aniseed, cinnamon, citron, and Barbadoes waters, together with ratafia and the most noble spirit of clary. But for cowslip-wine, poppy-water, and all dormitives, those I allow. – These provisos admitted, in other things I may prove a tractable and complying husband.

MILLAMANT O horrid provisos! Filthy strong waters! I toast fellows, odious men! I hate your odious provisos.

MIRABELL Then we're agreed. Shall I kiss your hand upon the contract? And here comes one to be a witness to the sealing of the deed.

[*Enter* MRS FAINALL.]

MILLAMANT Fainall, what shall I do? Shall I have him? I think I must have him.

MRS FAINALL Ay, ay, take him, take him. What should you do?

MILLAMANT Well then – I'll take my death I'm in a horrid fright – Fainall, I shall never say it – Well, I think – I'll endure you.

MRS FAINALL Fie, fie, have him, have him, and tell him so in plain terms, for I am sure you have a mind to him.

MILLAMANT Are you? I think I have, and the horrid man looks as if he thought so too. Well, you ridiculous thing you, I'll have you – I won't be kissed, nor I won't be thanked. Here, kiss my hand though. So, hold your tongue now, and don't say a word.

MRS FAINALL Mirabell, there's a necessity for your obedience; you have neither time to talk nor stay. My mother is coming; and in my conscience, if she should see you, would fall into fits, and maybe not recover time enough to return to Sir Rowland, who, as Foible tells me, is in a fair way to succeed. Therefore, spare your ecstasies for another occasion, and slip down the back stairs, where Foible waits to consult you.

MILLAMANT Ay, go, go. In the meantime I suppose you have said something to please me.

MIRABELL I am all obedience. [*Exit.*]

MRS FAINALL Yonder Sir Wilfull's drunk; and so noisy that my mother has been forced to leave Sir Rowland to appease him; but he answers her only with singing and drinking. What they may have done by this time I know not, but Petulant and he were upon quarrelling as I came by.

MILLAMANT Well, if Mirabell should not make a good husband, I am a lost thing – for I find I love him violently.

SAINT-SIMON

❧

His Nuptials

The day of my marriage was now fast approaching. During the previous year, there had been some talk of an alliance with the eldest daughter of the Maréchal de Lorges, but the idea had been dismissed almost as soon as entertained. Now, on both sides, there were great hopes of renewal. The Maréchal had been ruined in the wars, his only reward having been his marshal's bâton. As soon as he had received it, however, he had married the daughter of Frémont, the keeper of the King's jewels, who amassed a vast fortune under M. Colbert and was considered the ablest and most consulted financier of his day. Immediately after his marriage, the Maréchal had been appointed captain of the bodyguard, a post left vacant by the death of the Maréchal de Rochefort, and had earned a reputation for honour, courage and ability in that service.

The Maréchal de Lorges' integrity and candour had much pleased me when I had had the opportunity of observing him closely during the campaign which I fought under his command. The love and esteem in which he was held by the whole army, his high reputation at Court, his magnificent establishment and extremely noble birth, his distinguished connections that offset the inferior marriage which he was first in his line to be obliged to contract, all made me earnestly desire the match. His eldest brother, moreover, was greatly esteemed and, by a strange coincidence, held similar honours, offices and establishments. The devoted affection between them and, indeed, throughout the entire large family, most of all, the goodness and sincerity of the Maréchal himself, so rare, so real in him, made me very eager. I hoped to find everything that I lacked to sustain me and advance my interest and to enable me to live agreeably amid noble connections and a pleasant family.

What is more, in the irreproachable virtue of the Maréchal's wife, and her sagacity in reconciling her husband with M. de Louvois and thus gaining him a dukedom, I found everything that I could desire for training a wife whom I wished to appear at Court. There the Maréchale was universally praised and respected for the elegant, wise and dignified manner in which she kept open house to the highest society, without admixture, conducting herself with perfect modesty, yet never forgetting the position due to her husband's rank. By this means she had made her inferior birth forgotten by the Maréchal's family, the Court and society in general, where her character had earned her general esteem. Nevertheless, she existed only for her husband, who trusted her in everything and lived with her and all her relations in a mutual affection and respect that did him much credit.

They had one son, a boy of twelve whom they loved to distraction, and five daughters. The two elder had spent their childhood with the Benedictines, at Conflans, and for the past three years had been living with their grandmother, Mme Frémont, whose house communicated with that of the Maréchale de Lorges. The elder girl was seventeen, the second fifteen years old. They had never been allowed out of their grandmother's sight, for she was a woman of great good sense and perfect virtue, who, in her youth, had been exceedingly handsome and still retained some traces of her former beauty. She was a most pious lady, active in good works and entirely devoted to the upbringing of her two granddaughters. For a long time past her husband had been afflicted by paralysis and other diseases, but his mind was clear and he managed his own affairs. The Maréchale lived with them all, busy with all manner of duties and charities, and they respected her and loved her dearly.

Mme Frémont secretly preferred Mlle de Lorges, whereas the Maréchale's favourite was the second daughter, Mlle de Quintin. Indeed, had it depended only on her mother's wishes, the elder would have been sent to a convent in order to give her sister the chance of a better marriage. The latter had dark hair and beautiful eyes; Mlle de Lorges, on the other hand, was fair, with a perfect figure and complexion. She had a most pleasing expression, was very modest, yet stately in her bearing, and there was something about her that I thought very gracious because it came from natural goodness and gentleness. I liked her infinitely the better of the two when I first saw them together; there was no comparison for me, and I hoped that she would make my life's happiness, as she has done, solely and absolutely. As she is now my wife, I shall abstain from saying more, except that she has proved far above all that was promised me and beyond my own fondest hopes.

My mother and I were informed of all the necessary details by Mme Frémont's sister-in-law, a fine handsome woman, on excellent terms with them all and better used to good society than is usual with people of such inferior birth. She negotiated the marriage contract and skilfully but honestly steered matters to a successful conclusion, in spite of the obstacles that invariably beset life's most important occasions. Finally, however, all the difficulties were smoothed away for a consideration of four hundred thousand livres, cash down (with no concessions), and living expenses for an indefinite period at Court and with the army.

When the arrangements were at last completed, the Maréchal de Lorges spoke to the King, on my behalf as well as his own, to avoid trouble. His Majesty was gracious enough to say that he could not do better for his daughter, and went on to speak most kindly of me – the Maréchal enjoyed telling me this.

Thus it was that on the Thursday before Palm Sunday we signed the preliminary articles. Two days later, however, after we had taken the contract to the King and I was beginning to visit the Hôtel de Lorges every evening, the match was suddenly broken off on an ill-defined pretext, which everyone persisted in interpreting after his own fashion. Luckily, just as we had reached a deadlock, with everyone pulling in a different direction, d'Auneuil, the Maître des Requêtes, the Maréchale's only brother, arrived from the country where he had been on circuit and removed the obstacle at his own expense. (This is an obligation which I must repay and for which I shall ever be deeply grateful.) God sometimes uses the most unexpected means to carry out His will. The whole venture thus almost miscarried, but the marriage was at last celebrated at the Hôtel de Lorges, on 8 April, which I have always regarded, and with good reason, as the happiest day of my life. My mother behaved like the best of mothers. We proceeded to the Hôtel de Lorges on the Thursday before Low Sunday, at seven in the evening. The contract was signed and a grand banquet was given for the nearest relations on both sides of the family. At midnight, the curé of Saint-Roche said mass and we were married in the private chapel. On the previous evening, my mother had sent forty thousand livres' worth of jewels to Mlle de Lorges, and I a corbeille containing six

33

hundred louis and the elegant trifles usually given on such occasions.

We slept that night in the state bedroom and on the following day M. d'Auneuil, who lodged over the way, gave a great dinner for us, after which the bride received in her bed at the Hôtel de Lorges. The highest society of France came in great numbers out of civility and curiosity, and the first to arrive was the Duchesse de Bracciano and her two daughters. My mother was still in half-mourning, her apartments were draped with grey and black, which was why we preferred to receive the company at the Hôtel de Lorges. Only one day was devoted to these visits and on the following we went to Versailles. In the evening the King graciously asked to see the bride in Mme de Maintenon's apartments, where she was presented by my mother and by hers. The King joked with me about my marriage on the way, and was so obliging as to receive the ladies with much praise and distinction.

Afterwards they attended the King's supper, and the new duchess had her tabouret. As he came to the table, the King said to her, 'Madame, pray be seated.' He looked up as his napkin was being unfolded and, seeing all the duchesses and princesses still standing, he half-rose from his chair and said to Mme de Saint-Simon, 'Madame, I have already asked you to be seated,' whereupon all those who had the right sat down, and Mme de Saint-Simon sat between my mother and hers, who came after her in order of rank.

Next day, she received the entire Court, in her bed, in the apartments of the Duchesse d'Arpajon, as being most convenient because they were on the ground floor. The Maréchal de Lorges and I were present only for the visit of the royal family. On the day after, they went to Saint-Germain and on to Paris, where I gave a grand dinner at my house for the whole wedding party. On the following day I gave a private supper to those remaining of my father's old friends, to whom I had been careful to announce my marriage before it was made public, and whom I always took great pains to cultivate until the day of their death.

E. M. ALMEDINGEN

from *So Dark a Stream*

In mid-July Paul wrote to his mother:

> . . . I find the princess well enough, tall, good-looking, not
> shy . . . My choice is made. She is most intelligent, and has
> studied geometry, and tells me such knowledge is necessary
> for clear reasoning. Her manners are unaffected, she likes
> staying at home, is fond of music and reading, and longs to
> start learning Russian.

A little later the Grand-Duke said that his fiancée had
already mastered 'our alphabet', and Catherine was delighted. 'Your letters are a joy. I am expecting you back most
impatiently . . .'

There was not – and there could not be – a breath of any
personal attachment. He had found Sophie Dorothea 'well
enough'. She was of blood royal, had neither hare-lip nor
squint, and very thorough and confidential inquiries had
established her perfect fitness of muscle and bone. Paul did
not know that he came to her as a deliverer. Sophie
Dorothea had had no voice in the matter of her engagement
to Ludwig of Darmstadt. Yet she knew quite enough about
his habits. She must marry where she was bid. But the
future, now opening to her, was so unimaginably splendid
that in a mood of candour she admitted her high good

fortune in a telling enough phrase when writing to an intimate friend: *'J'ai eu le pas sur toutes les princesses et altesses impériales.'*

Rather coldly, as though he were desirous not to lessen the distance between them, the Grand-Duke – on the eve of his leaving for Russia, presented his fiancée with an odd document purporting to embody points of guidance for her behaviour at the Russian Court.

> I do not mean to speak about love . . . that would depend on circumstances . . . The Princess will have to exercise her patience and gentleness to endure my temper, my variable moods, and my impatience . . . The Princess must not interfere in State matters . . . She must never accept any advice from the members of the household . . . It will be necessary for her so to frame her behaviour as to exclude the least possibility of being involved in intrigues . . .

The fourteen heavily-worded clauses might have pleased a serjeant-major in the Prussian army. Paul was twenty-two at the time, but the substance of the paper seems to have been struck from a middle-aged mint. Indeed, the results of Paul's first sojourn in Prussia would have delighted Peter III. King Frederick having entertained his guest with endless reviews and manoeuvres, the Grand-Duke now felt irresistibly drawn to a landscape laid out with monotony, orderliness and severity. He would return to St Petersburg, a Prussophile to his finger-tips, all his earlier blind preferences confirmed by the evidences of his senses. Once again, however unwittingly, the Empress had been instrumental in widening the gulf between them.

The pompous paper in no way disturbed Sophie Dorothea, who is said to have learned all the fourteen clauses by heart. Again, for all her lack of experience, she must have known Paul was not in the least in love with her, but that did not prevent her from pouring her heart out to him.

37

She was proud and ambitious. She was also candid as Paul would learn soon after her arrival in Russia.

Meanwhile, he hurried back to the north to find his mother satisfied, the Court congratulatory, and the entire capital flung into a vortex of urgent preparations for the wedding. The Princess was expected in September, and nothing was spared in energy, labour, money, or affection to enhance the national pleasure at her arrival. Two palaces in St Petersburg were entirely refurnished. The grand-ducal apartments at Tsarskoe Selo were set out with a blinding luxury. The slow means of transport considered, the achievement suggests a truly Herculean energy.

Sophie Dorothea came, determined to make friends, and she succeeded almost instantly. They called her a prodigy. At so early a stage not only had she mastered the Russian alphabet but she had learned enough to speak her greetings in Russian.

Events moved rapidly. Within a week, received into the Russian Church, Sophie Dorothea became Grand-Duchess Marie. Her betrothal followed immediately. In the evening of that day, Paul's ring on her left hand, she wrote the most impassioned letter he had ever received:

Most solemnly do I vow to love and to worship you. Nothing in the world would ever change me . . . Such are the feelings of your devoted and most faithful friend and fiancée, Maria Feodorowna.

The Grand-Duke would not discuss love. But he could not prevent her adoration. The girl of seventeen, fond of music and mathematics, chose to confirm her vows before her wedding-day, and the passionate promise would be kept to the end, though she could not have foreseen the bitter and rigorous tests her rock-like loyalty and her vehement love would have to face.

It was indeed vehement. There is something of Latin abandon in the letters of that staidly bred girl from Württemberg. They blaze, they shine, almost they blind. She would be restrained and dignified with others – but never with Paul.

My adored, dearest Prince [she wrote some few days before their marriage], I cannot go to bed without telling you once again that I love you unto madness ... God knows what happiness it will be to belong to you wholly, and that so soon. My entire life will serve as a proof of my love. Good-night, dearest Prince, sleep well, don't let any nightmares disturb you. Think a little of her who adores you. Marie.

ANONYMOUS

Sukey, you shall be my wife
   And I will tell you why:
I have got a little pig,
   And you have got a sty;
I have got a dun cow
   And you can make good cheese;
Sukey, will you marry me?
   Say Yes, if you please.

JANE AUSTEN

♥

from *Sense and Sensibility*

'A woman of seven and twenty,' said Marianne, after pausing a moment, 'can never hope to feel or inspire affection again, and if her home be uncomfortable, or her fortune small, I can suppose that she might bring herself to submit to the offices of a nurse, for the sake of the provision and security of a wife. In his marrying such a woman therefore there would be nothing unsuitable. It would be a compact of convenience, and the world would be satisfied. In my eyes it would be no marriage at all, but that would be nothing. To me it would seem only a commercial exchange, in which each wished to be benefited at the expense of the other.'

IRIS ORIGO

❧

from *The Last Attachment*

*On ne saurait s'y prendre de trop de façons, et par trop de bouts,
pour connaître un homme.*

Sainte-Beuve

On the happy occasion of the Espousals arranged and
concluded between the Cavaliere Commendatore Alessandro
Guiccioli and the Contessa Teresa Gamba Ghiselli daughter
of Conte Ruggero, both of this city, it has been thought
desirable to put on record the dowry assigned by Conte
Ruggero to his aforesaid Daughter, as well as to establish the
rules that will govern their future union . . .

In view of the Marriage Conte Ruggero Gamba Ghiselli,
having come before this Notary Public and in the presence of
Witnesses . . . has assigned and made over to his Daughter
Contessa Teresa the dowry of scudi 4500 . . .

The Cavaliere promises and guarantees to his Spouse the
Contessa in case of her Widowhood – which God avert – a
decent and comfortable provision from the Guiccioli Fortune,
so long as she lives a Widow's life, and the interest on her
dowry remains with the Guiccioli family . . .

This marriage contract, drawn up in the little provincial
town of Ravenna in the Romagna, on 20 January 1818, is
the beginning of the story.

Forty years lay between the bride and bridegroom, and they had met for the first time three months before, when the bride had just come home from school. The second of Count Gamba's five pretty daughters, she was, by all accounts, the most attractive, and moreover the prize pupil of S Chiara, the new-fangled convent school at Faenza – which had been opened during the recent French domination. Here – although she was something of a little hoyden, quick-tempered and vain and, her schoolfellows whispered, extremely ambitious – Teresa had received an education exceptional for a girl of her time. The abbess, Madre Rampi – a woman of great character – had decided to create a model establishment, in which girls (almost as if they were boys) would be given *une éducation forte*, comprising not only an appreciation of the classic authors of their own language, but a thorough training in the arts of eloquence and rhetoric. The school, indeed, was closed a few years later by the Church, on the grounds that so much learning was dangerous for women; but meanwhile its pupils had learned how to hold a conversation about Dante or Petrarch, and how to write letters in a style from which every trace of simplicity and naturalness was eliminated. Moreover at home Teresa had also enjoyed the teaching of her brother's professor, Paolo Costa, who had imparted to her, as well as a love of literature, the rudiments of philosophy. She was, in short, a very well-educated young lady indeed, and aware of it; and perhaps this helped her to face with equanimity the prospect of marriage with a man who, whatever his faults (and it is not likely that much of the gossip had reached her ears), was known to be the wittiest and most cultivated man in Ravenna, who had been a friend of Alfieri's, and was a patron of the theatre. Teresa, her sisters whispered enviously, would have her own box at the Opera – had not the Ravenna theatre been restored largely at the Count's expense? – she would have a fine

43

house, with many servants in livery, including two 'mori' in rich Oriental costumes, with pistols and daggers at their belts; she would drive in the Carnival cavalcade in a coach-and-six preceded by outriders with blue and white feathers in their caps. Besides, says the Count's grandson, 'my grandfather was a handsome man, vigorous, rich, intelligent, agreeable in conversation, skilled in seduction, of fine manners and illustrious family.' What more could a girl desire? And so, on a late autumn evening of the year 1817, a curious little scene took place in the drawing-room of Palazzo Gamba.

A gentle, blushing girl of eighteen – with a poor figure, but a brilliant complexion and a mass of lovely auburn hair, stood in the middle of the room, curtsying, as her father introduced her to a rigid elderly man with red hair and whiskers, whom she had never seen before. The room was ill-lit, and the future bridegroom was short-sighted.

Without a word, he took a candle in his hand, and with a faint smile on his thin lips he slowly walked round the girl, examining her points 'as if about to buy a piece of furniture'. The next day the bargain was concluded.

EDWARD LEAR

'The Owl and the Pussy-Cat'

The Owl and the Pussy-Cat went to sea
   In a beautiful pea-green boat:
They took some honey, and plenty of money
   Wrapped up in a five-pound note.
The Owl looked up to the stars above,
   And sang to a small guitar,
'O lovely Pussy, O Pussy, my love,
What a beautiful Pussy you are,
          You are,
          You are!
What a beautiful Pussy you are!

Pussy said to the Owl, 'You elegant fowl,
   How charmingly sweet you sing!
Oh! let us be married; too long we have tarried:
   But what shall we do for a ring?
They sailed away, for a year and a day
   To the land where the Bong-tree grows,
And there in a wood a Piggy-wig stood,
With a ring at the end of his nose,
          His nose,
          His nose!
With a ring at the end of his nose.

'Dear Pig, are you willing to sell for one shilling
    Your ring?' Said the Piggy, 'I will.'
So they took it away, and were married next day
    By the Turkey who lives on the hill.
They dined on mince, and slices of quince,
    Which they ate with a runcible spoon;
And hand in hand, on the edge of the sand,
They danced by the light of the moon,
                        The moon,
                        The moon,
They danced by the light of the moon.

PART TWO

Loss

INTRODUCTION

I have put this part here because there is no chronology about loss. People can be torn from each other for many other reasons than age: the Raleghs by politics, the Woolfs by mental anguish, the Stockwells by war, the Partridges and the Lewises by illness. Only the Browns were forced apart because they were old and weak and *poor*; authoritarian 'kindness' killed them, much as it does today by separating so many single, old, weak and poor people from their cat or their dog, the only living creature who gives and takes their love.

There are two epitaphs and Emma Bovary's father's touching reminiscence of his loss. Loss, like love, can strike where it chooses – nobody is immune. There is Thomas Carlyle's moving tribute to his dead wife, full of those agonising regrets at not having communicated his love and regard for her that many of us will recognise with a sad familiarity. Who has not lost a parent or a grandparent without afterwards feeling something of the kind? People, as George Eliot said, not only need to be loved, they need to be *told* that they are loved. Presumptions are always unrewarding and often downright dangerous. The willow cabin is infinitely preferable to the monument.

SIR HENRY WOTTON

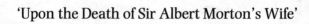

'Upon the Death of Sir Albert Morton's Wife'

He first deceas'd; she for a little tried
To live without him: lik'd it not, and died.

SIR WALTER RALEGH

❥

Letter to his wife, 1603

You shall now receive (my deare wife) my last words in
these my last lines. My love I send you that you may keep
it when I am dead, and my councell that you may
remember it when I am no more. I would not by my will
present you with sorrowes (dear Besse) let them go to the
grave with me and be buried in the dust. And seeing that it
is not Gods will that I should see you any more in this life,
beare it patiently, and with a heart like thy selfe.

First, I send you all the thankes which my heart can
conceive, or my words can reherse for your many
travailes, and care taken for me, which though they have
not taken effect as you wished, yet my debt to you is not
the lesse: but pay it I never shall in this world.

Secondly, I beseech you for the love you beare me living,
do not hide your selfe many dayes, but by your travailes
seeke to helpe your miserable fortunes and the right of
your poor childe. Thy mourning cannot availe me, I am
but dust.

Thirdly, you shall understand, that my land was conveyed *bona fide* to my childe; the writings were drawne at
midsummer was twelve months, my honest cosen Brett
can testify so much, and Dolberry too, can remember
somewhat therein. And I trust my blood will quench their

malice that have cruelly murthered me: and that they will not seek also to kill thee and thine with extreame poverty.

To what friend to direct thee I know not, for all mine have left me in the true time of tryall. And I perceive that my death was determined from the first day. Most sorry I am God knowes that being thus surprised with death I can leave you in no better estate. God is my witnesse I meant you all my office of wines or all that I could have purchased by selling it, halfe of my stuffe, and all my jewels, but some one for the boy, but God hath prevented all my resolutions. That great God that ruleth all in all, but if you live free from want, care for no more, for the rest is but vanity. Love God, and begin betimes to repose your selfe upon him, and therein shall you finde true and lasting riches, and endlesse comfort: for the rest when you have travailed and wearied your thoughts over all sorts of worldly cogitations, you shall but sit downe by sorrowe in the end.

Teach your son also to love and feare God while he is yet young, that the feare of God may grow with him, and then God will be a husband to you, and a father to him; a husband and a father which cannot be taken from you.

Baily oweth me 200 pounds, and Adrian Gilbert 600. In Jersey I also have much owing me besides. The arrearages of the wines will pay my debts. And howsoever you do, for my soules sake, pay all poore men. When I am gone, no doubt you shall be sought for by many, for the world thinkes that I was very rich. But take heed of the pretences of men, and their affections, for they last not but in honest and worthy men, and no greater misery can befall you in this life, than to become a prey, and afterwards to be despised. I speake not this (God knowes) to dissuade you from marriage, for it will be best for you, both in respect of the world and of God. As for me, I am no more yours, nor you mine, death hath cut us asunder: and God hath divided me from the world, and you from me.

Remember your poor childe for his father's sake, who chose you, and loved you in his happiest times. Get those letters (if it be possible) which I writ to the lords, wherein I sued for my life: God is my witnesse it was for you and yours that I desired life, but it is true that I distained my self for begging of it: for know it (my deare wife) that your son is the son of a true man, and one who in his owne respect despiseth death and all his misshapen & ugly formes.

I cannot write much, God he knows how hardly I steale this time while others sleep, and it is also time that I should separate my thoughts from the world. Begg my dead body which living denied thee; and either lay it at Sherburne (and if the land continue) or in Exeter-Church, by my Father and Mother; I can say no more, time and death call me away.

The everlasting God, powerfull, infinite, and omnipotent God, that Almighty God, who is goodnesse it selfe, the true life and true light keep thee and thine: have mercy on me, and teach me to forgive my persecutors and false accusers, and send us to meet in his glorious Kingdome. My deare wife farewell. Blesse my poore boy. Pray for me, and let my good God hold you both in his armes.

Written with the dying hand of sometimes thy Husband, but now alasse overthrowne.

Yours that was, but now not my own.
Walter Ralegh

VIRGINIA WOOLF

'My Husband Lives in That House'

In the early 1930s, years after her marriage, Virginia Woolf was talking with an old friend, Bobo Mayer, who remembered the conversation thus:

[she] said – and as though addressing herself rather than me: 'What do you think is probably the happiest moment in one's whole life?' While I was wondering how I should answer this sudden question, she went on, with a strange but very quiet radiance in her voice: 'I think it's the moment when one is walking in one's garden, perhaps picking off a few dead flowers, and suddenly one thinks: My husband lives in that house – and he loves me.' Her face shone as I had never seen it.

LEONARD WOOLF

'Come to Tea and Let Us Comfort You'

On the day of Virginia Woolf's death, after all efforts to find her had failed, Leonard wrote a note which, creased and worn, was found among his effects when he died twenty-eight years later. It read:

They said: 'Come to tea and let us comfort you.' But it's no good. One must be crucified on one's own private cross.

It is a strange fact that a terrible pain in the heart can be interrupted by a little pain in the fourth toe of the right foot.

I know that V. will not come across the garden from the lodge, and yet I look in that direction for her. I know that she is drowned and yet I listen for her to come in at the door. I know that it is the last page and yet I turn it over. There is no limit to one's own stupidity and selfishness.

from *Last Letters Home*

Laurie Stockwell met Gwenyth Crow when they were at school. He went to the boys' grammar at Hampton, she to the girls' at Twickenham. Both were very keen swimmers. Gwenyth was even put up for the Olympics, but her father wouldn't let her try for them. They had other boyfriends and girlfriends while they were growing up, but not long after leaving school, in 1939, they decided to get married. 'We got married in Oxford, very much against our parents' wishes. His parents were horrified, mine gave their consent unwillingly. We had dinner at the Randolph afterwards with all our RAF friends, everyone got very drunk.'

Laurie had only gone into the RAF at the end of 1939 to do his training. He had volunteered in 1938, but because he was a civil servant he wasn't released until 1939. Gwenyth stayed at home with her parents to begin with, but once Laurie became a flying instructor, they rented a house in Shawbury in Shropshire. 'We had an incredible life, in the heart of the country, but with a wonderful social life. We met lots of young people, dined in the mess, danced, and certainly didn't realise there was a food shortage. I was twenty, Laurie was twenty-two.'

In the middle of 1942 their social life and their life together came to an abrupt end. Laurie volunteered for

Bomber Command. Wives were not permitted to live within a thirty-mile radius of where their husbands were stationed. Gwen went back to her parents.

Laurie and Gwen hated being apart. In one undated letter, when he was still training, he wrote telling her how lonely life was without her:

> Thank you for the pullover which is also a great success. Thank you for marrying me. No, I'm not going mad, I just feel like thanking you for everything. You have made life so very much happier for me knowing that you are by my side always.
>
> I've been feeling very sad lately however. Spring is showing signs of breaking forth and it has made the empty space feel even emptier, the space, of course is the one you usually take up . . .

'He wanted to get into Pathfinders. Everyone knew it was a one-way ticket. Why do men do these things? I can remember now his excitement, but it was the end of the world for me, my heart was in my boots. I tried not to show it. Well, you can imagine what I thought. Only the *crème de la crème* were accepted. They were all volunteers. He was aware after each leave that we might never see each other again, but I never tried to dissuade him.'

Laurie joined at the beginning of December 1942. 'The only way I knew whether Laurie was on "ops" on Bomber Command was that they were always given a pint of milk for dinner the night before, and he would write and tell me when he'd had milk.'

On the night of 17 January 1943 Laurie flew out on a bombing raid over Berlin. By the following morning he had been reported missing. Gwen was eight months pregnant. The next day a letter came from his commanding officer.

RAF, Station Wigsley
Nr Newark
Nottinghamshire
18 January 1943

Mrs G. H. Stockwell
87 Fairfax Road
Teddington
Middlesex

Dear Mrs Stockwell

It is with regret that I have to corroborate my telegram concerning your husband who is missing from an operation on the night of 17th–18th January 1943.

Your husband was one of our most reliable and popular Officers, and his absence will be greatly felt by his fellow Officers.

If I receive any further information, you can be assured that I will let you know immediately.

Yours very sincerely

Group Captain, Commanding,

RAF, Station Wigsley

Five months later another letter came from the Air Ministry:

Air Ministry
(Casualty Branch)
73–77 Oxford Street
London W1
29 May 1943

Madam

I am directed to refer to a letter from this Department dated 24th January 1943, and to inform you with regret that no news has been received of your husband, Flying Officer Laurence Edwin Stockwell, since he was reported missing on the night of 17th/18th January 1943.

The detailed report from his Squadron states that his aircraft set out at 4.27 p.m. to attack an objective at Berlin. At 9.52 p.m. its approximate position was estimated to be in the vicinity of Utrecht, Holland, and at 10.20 p.m. its position was off the west coast of Holland. No news of it or of any of its occupants has since become available from any source.

In view of the time which has elapsed it is felt that there can now be little hope that your husband is alive, but action to presume his death will not be taken until at least six months from the date on which he was reported missing. Such action would then be for official purposes only, and a further letter would be addressed to you before it was taken.

I am to express the Department's deep sympathy with you in your great anxiety, and to assure you that enquiries are continuing through the International Red Cross Committee and any news later received will be immediately passed to you.

I am, Madam,

Your obedient servant

Gwen remembers the day the telegram arrived: 'My mother was away and my father was at work. I took the dog out for a walk. When I returned, the telegram was on the mat. The Pathfinders always went ahead on any mission, and stayed the longest over the target to protect the other planes. He had got to Berlin, but I later found out the mission had been totally abortive, they had bombed the suburbs and missed the target.

'We were so close there was nothing else I could do but encourage him, but what I really wanted to say was "What about our unborn baby?" He was thrilled about my being pregnant, I knew it was going to be a girl. Laurie had come to the doctor with me on his last leave, and the doctor had turned to him and said, "Don't worry, old chap, I'll look after her." And he did. It was my saving I think. I was determined from the moment I heard about Laurie that it wasn't going to affect the baby. Everyone else thought she'd come on January 19th, she didn't, she came on February 23rd. Both our parents were fantastically supportive.'

Gwen had written to Laurie every day, sometimes twice a day. 'I wanted to keep him in touch with home, however mundane it was. Our letters were an anchor. They were the most important thing in one's life at the time, we just waited for the postman. All my letters to him came back after he was missing. I burnt them all, they were such drivel.'

Laurie had written whenever he could, but it was impossible to write every day if you were in Pathfinders. His last letter arrived two days after he was killed.

Officers' Mess
Royal Air Force
Wigsley
Newark
Notts
15–1–43

Tel: Spalford

Gwen Darling
Please forgive me for not writing these last two days, there is no excuse whatsoever, I've just been a bit browned off, that's all, but as that feeling has passed, everything is O.K. As two of your letters arrived together today, one saying about your fears a few days ago and the other about mother telling you that you should not have told me, and also that it was a false alarm, I was quite happy about things, but please take no notice of mother and tell me everything for I feel much happier if I know what is going on.

The nursery furniture looks quite good. I'd try and get what you can of it. Please forgive me for a terribly short note.

By the way one item of news, or two rather. First I have at last had a receipt from Heyford after threatening to stop payment of the cheque and secondly, we also get a pint of milk nowadays, a glass at breakfast and one at tea.

All my love Darling

Yours always

Laurie

However, Laurie had also written Gwen a letter early in 1942 which is, in sentiment and intent, very much a last letter. It is the one that Gwen has treasured most. Laurie had said he would be a conscientious objector before the war; he had cried at the time of saying it at the mere thought of war. This letter synthesises her feeling about all that he held dear and important. Gwen says that she knew every sentiment in it before she got it: 'I knew anyway, knew exactly how he thought, and he me, it was one of those incredible things we had from childhood. The neighbours used to say, "It's all wrong that those two should be parted." He didn't accept anything. It seems like it's written by someone young because it's so optimistic. Knowing what one knows now, it would be so difficult to write back to it now.'

Sunday

My Darling

When I was walking back from Heyford Station yesterday, I realised how little I appreciated the beauty of the country-side, how little I seemed to take interest, and on realising that I stopped in the road and looked about me, and for the first time noticed how lovely everything is about here. Having found that out I tried to fathom the question of why I hadn't noticed it before, why I wasn't taking my usual interest in the countryside, for although I'm not of a poetic nature or anything like it, I feel that I've always taken quite a lot of interest in my surroundings, I loved the Isle of Wight and all the places of natural beauty, especially St Martha's which holds such wonderful memories for me. And I came to these conclusions. Firstly, this beastly war. War has no rightful place on this earth, besides destroying men and property, everything that is seen, it destroys those unseen things, our senses, our sense of beauty, happiness, comradeship amongst all men, anything that is worth living for. Property is not essential. But happiness, a love of beauty, friendship between all peoples and individuals, is life itself.

Secondly, you. I've put you second, I wonder if you feel that strange. But this war affects everybody, I'd be very selfish if I put you first in this thought, I'm trying to fathom out for myself. You are just everything to me. The unforgivable way I write would make another feel that you have been guilty of my loss in taking no notice in the surrounding beauty, but you understand, I'm sure, that it is only because I'm not constantly with you, that is the real factor. You, Darling, have made me able to see, to feel and to understand, all the beauty that is in the world, and life itself, without you that understanding does not disappear, for you are with me constantly, in my thoughts, but that understanding of life does seem to fade.

This war is keeping us apart, and therefore it is to blame in my loss, and that loss is not only mine but of every person in the world connected with the war.

I have never spoken to you of my feelings and thoughts about this war, and I hope I will never speak of them again. Do you remember a small boy saying he would be a conscientious objector if war came? Things happened to change that small boy's views, talk of brutality, human suffering, atrocities, but that did not have any great effect on changing my mind for I realise that we all are capable of doing these deeds of which we read so much nowadays. It is

61

the fact that a few people wish to take freedom from the peoples of the earth that changed my views. News of atrocities only breeds hate, and hate is contemptible in my eyes. I will never be capable I hope of hating anyone whatever they have done.

Why should I then fight in the war which only brings disgust into my thoughts?

It is so that I might live in happiness and peace all my days with you. You notice I put myself first, again it is a strange thing but I am trying hard to be honest with myself and I find that I, and consequently everybody, am terribly selfish, it is human nature, I'm afraid.

I am also fighting so that one day happiness will again rule the world, and with happiness that love of beauty, of life, contentment, fellowship among all men may return. You may again have noticed that I have not mentioned fighting for one's country, for the empire, that to me is just foolishness, for greatness in one nation will always breed hate and longing in another, and the whole of life will again be disrupted.

Mainly, however, I'm fighting for the freedom of all men, and in that I am fighting just as much for the Germans as for the English people. With freedom and the destruction of hate this world will enter into a period which I hope will be much in advance of anything it has ever known.

When peace returns, and may it soon, the world must make sure that the men and women of the future are educated in the right way, a love of beauty, not a love of war, and it is our own job to teach our children about all the loveliness of this world, to make them happy so that they can understand that love and happiness are the things really worth having.

Well, Darling, I seem to have been rambling on for some time, really I must stop. I don't know whether I have made any sense out of my ramblings, I only hope so.

Today's news is very small. I saw *They Flew Alone* tonight, and I think I enjoyed it, I'm not quite sure.

The Stars Look Down although not a pleasant sort of book has held my interest and I'm reading solidly through it.

All my love, Darling, you mean so very much to me

Always

Laurie

Gwen has never been back to Shawbury, or Shrewsbury, since Laurie died: 'I couldn't, I want to remember it as it was.' She had been living in a little village called Battlefield, and when her daughter Anne Marie was born, she went back there for eighteen months. 'It was hell going back to the same house. We were outside the village and completely isolated.'

FRANCES PARTRIDGE

꘎

from *Everything to Lose: Diaries 1945–1960*

May 4th 1948. I quite often look back at the pleasures and pains of youth – love, jealousy, recklessness, vanity – without forgetting their spell but no longer desiring them; while middle-aged ones like music, places, botany, conversation seem to be just as enjoyable as those wilder ones, in which there was usually some potential anguish lying in wait, like a bee in a flower. I hope there may be further surprises in store, and on the whole do not fear the advance into age . . .

May 5th. Ralph to London to the dentist. I have sprained my ankle so cannot go with him but as the years pass I *hate* being parted from him even for an hour or so; I feel only half a person by myself, with one arm, one leg and half a face.

Warmer, softer, sweeter day: the birds sing very loudly and the pollarded trees on the road to Hungerford station seem to be holding little bunches of greenery in their fists.

On her husband's death

November 28th 1960. Last night before dinner I missed Ralph for a while. For the thousandth time I wondered, 'Is he all right? Could he perhaps be feeling ill?' Usually after the first panic and wild wobblings on my base, my equilibrium has been restored. This time, however, I felt it was odd that he should be in the library at this cold evening hour. I ran upstairs and found him lying down. No, he was *not* all right. Going through the kitchen to look at the stove he had suddenly felt a constriction in the chest, like two bars. He took a pill and then another, but remained limp and drowsy, wanting no food and unable to face the company. I am in a spurious way so armoured against these set-backs that a dreadful unearthly calm settled down on me, partly to make me able to face his dread of my 'fussing'. But along with this grey tristesse was the awareness of a huge crater opening, black and menacing. Paralysed in mind and hardly able to talk, I went downstairs and cooked dinner and somehow sketched in a part in the conversation until the meal was over, when I was able to go up and lie beside Ralph.

This morning he swears he is better, but is in no great hurry to get up. We must 'greet the unknown' with all possible commonsense, but I am full of doubts which I cannot voice to him.

November 29th. Throughout yesterday I sank slowly into the pit, as it became gradually clear to me that 'something or other' did happen in the stove-room on Sunday night. Ralph was comatose and fighting a desperate rearguard action against admitting himself ill. He beomes furious (frighteningly so, because it is bad for him) if I treat him as such, and I identify myself so completely with him that the difficulty of overriding the line he has decided to take is almost insuperable . . .

November 30th. But last night was much worse than my fears. I dropped into exhausted sleep. but soon awoke and listened to Ralph's struggling breathing for four hours, while the clock snailed round its course. But why describe such agony? We are both alive this morning – that's all I can say.

Morning calls to Red-beard and Geoff, visits from Red-beard – but I have antagonised him, I see. There is something so futile about him, and I couldn't bear the snobbish reluctance he showed to get into touch with the Reading Specialist who unfortunately happens to be a lord. Yet to some extent we depend on him, and I try to choke back my horror that this little mannikin should be relevant to the health and safety of my darling Ralph. I pressed on, screaming silently from every cranny of my brain, until I got him to arrange for the lordly cardiologist to come tomorrow. Geoff seemed to take things more seriously when I described Ralph's breathing. It seems that he took two sleeping pills while I dozed last night, one seeming insufficient, and Geoff thought this might have affected his breathing. He has recommended a new sort for tonight. I dashed in to Hungerford to get them. Not available. I have ordered them to be brought out by taxi from Newbury, and we have got them now.

Ralph does seem a little better this evening and with more appetite for his supper. He even read more. I went downstairs while he was eating, and listened to Berlioz's *Symphonie Fantastique* on the wireless without much pleasure. I left Ralph a walking-stick to bang on the floor if he wanted me – I never expected to hear, nor shall I ever forget that dreadful 'thump, thump, thump'.

December 1st. Now I am *absolutely alone and for ever.*

THOMAS CARLYLE

from *Reminiscences*

I doubt candidly, if I ever saw a nobler human soul than this which (alas, alas, never rightly valued till now!) accompanied all my steps for forty years. Blind and deaf that we are: oh, think, if thou yet love anybody living, wait not till death sweep down the paltry little dust-clouds and idle dissonances of the moment, and all be at last so mournfully clear and beautiful when it is too late!

She had from an early period formed her own little opinion about me (what an Eldorado to me, ungrateful being, blind, condemnable, and heavy laden, and crushed down into blindness by great misery as I oftenest was!), and she never flinched from it an instant, I think, or cared, or counted, what the world said to the contrary.

Ah me! she never knew fully, nor could I show her in my heavy-laden miserable life, how much I had at all times regarded, loved, and admired her. No telling of her now. 'Five minutes more of your dear company in this world. Oh that I had you yet for but five minutes, to tell you all!' This is often my thought since 21 April.

LAURIE LEE

♪

from *Cider with Rosie*

This is the author's recollection of an old couple who lived near his village in Gloucestershire.

But if you survived melancholia and rotting lungs it was possible to live long in this valley. Joseph and Hannah Brown, for instance, appeared to be indestructible. For as long as I could remember they had lived together in the same house up by the common. They had lived there, it was said, for fifty years; which seemed to me for ever. They had raised a large family and sent them into the world, and had continued to live on alone, with nothing left of their noisy brood save some dog-eared letters and photographs.

The old couple were as absorbed in themselves as lovers, content and self-contained; they never left the village or each other's company, they lived as snug as two podded chestnuts. By day blue smoke curled up from their chimney, at night the red windows glowed; the cottage, when we passed it, said 'Here live the Browns', as though that were part of nature.

Though white and withered, they were active enough, but they ordered their lives without haste. The old woman cooked, and threw grain to the chickens, and hung out her washing on bushes; the old man fetched wood and chopped it with a billhook, did a bit of gardening now and then, or just sat on a seat outside his door and gazed at the valley, or slept. When summer came they bottled fruit, and when winter came they ate it. They did nothing more than was necessary to live, but did it fondly, with skill – then sat together in their clock-ticking kitchen enjoying their half-century of silence. Whoever called to see them was welcomed gravely, be it man or beast or child; and to me they resembled two tawny insects, slow but deft in their movements; a little foraging, some frugal feeding, then any amount of stillness. They spoke to each other without raised voices, in short chirrups as brief as bird-song, and when they moved about in their tiny kitchen they did so smoothly and blind, gliding on worn, familiar rails, never bumping or obstructing each other. They were fond, pink-faced, and alike as cherries, having taken and merged, through their years together, each other's looks and accents.

It seemed that the old Browns belonged for ever, and that the miracle of their survival was made commonplace by the durability of their love – if one should call it love, such a balance. Then suddenly, within the space of two days, feebleness took them both. It was as though two machines, wound up and synchronised, had run down at exactly the same time. Their interdependence was so legendary we didn't notice their plight at first. But after a week, not having been seen about, some neighbours thought it best to call. They found old Hannah on the kitchen floor feeding her man with a spoon. He was lying in a corner half-covered with matting, and they were both too weak to stand. She had chopped up a plate of peelings, she said, as she hadn't been able to manage the fire. But they were all right really, just a touch of the damp; they'd do, and it didn't matter.

Well, the Authorities were told, the Visiting Spinsters got busy; and it was decided they would have to be moved.

69

They were too frail to help each other now, and their children were too scattered, too busy. There was but one thing to be done; it was for the best; they would have to be moved to the Workhouse.

The old couple were shocked and terrified, and lay clutching each other's hands. 'The Workhouse' – always a word of shame, grey shadow falling on the close of life, most feared by the old (even when called The Infirmary); abhorred more than debt, or prison, or beggary, or even the stain of madness.

Hannah and Joseph thanked the Visiting Spinsters but pleaded to be left at home, to be left as they wanted, to cause no trouble, just simply to stay together. The Workhouse could not give them the mercy they needed, but could only divide them in charity. Much better to hide, or die in a ditch, or to starve in one's familiar kitchen, watched by the objects one's life had gathered – the scrubbed empty table, the plates and saucepans, the cold grate, the white stopped clock . . .

'You'll be well looked after,' the Spinsters said, 'and you'll see each other twice a week.' The bright busy voices cajoled with authority and the old couple were not trained to defy them. So that same afternoon, white and speechless, they were taken away to the Workhouse. Hannah Brown was put to bed in the Woman's Wing, and Joseph lay in the Men's. It was the first time in all their fifty years, that they had ever been separated. They did not see each other again, for in a week they both were dead.

I was haunted by their end as by no other, and by the kind, killing Authority that arranged it. Divided, their life went out of them, so they ceased as by mutual agreement. Their cottage stood empty on the edge of the common, its front door locked and soundless. Its stones grew rapidly cold and repellent with its life so suddenly withdrawn. In a year it fell down, first the roof, then the walls, and lay

70

scattered in a tangle of briars. Its decay was so violent and overwhelming, it was as though the old couple had wrecked it themselves.

Soon all that remained of Joe and Hannah Brown, and of their long close life together, were some grass-grown stumps, a garden gone wild, some rusty pots, and a dog-rose.

Inscription in the church of St Andrew, Branfield, Suffolk 1737

❥

A memorial to Bridgett Applewhaite, 'once Bridgett Nelson',
bears the following words:

After the Fatigues of a married Life
Borne by Her with Incredible Patience
For four years and three quarters, bating three weeks
And after the enjoyment of Glorious Freedom
Of an Easy and unblemisht Widowhood
For four years and Upwards
She resolved to run the Risk of a Second Marriage Bed
But DEATH forbad the Banns
And having with an Apoplectick Dart
(The same instrument with which he had formerly dis-
    patcht her Mother)
Toucht the most vital part of her Brain
She must have fallen directly to the ground
(As one Thunder strook)
If she had not been catcht and supported
By her intended Husband
Of which invisible bruise
After a struggle for above sixty Hours
With that grand Enemy to Life
(But the Certain and Merciful Friend
to helpless Old Age)

In terrible Convulsions, Plaintive groans or Stupefying
   Sleep
Without recovery of Speech or Senses,
She dyed on the 12th day of Sept.
In ye year of our Lord 1737
                    of her own age 44.

GUSTAVE FLAUBERT

from *Madame Bovary*

*Père Rouault seeks to console his doctor, Charles Bovary, whose
wife has recently died.*

One morning old Rouault called to make the payment to
Charles for the setting of his leg: seventy-five francs in two-
franc pieces, and a turkey. He had heard of his bereavement
and offered the best consolation he could.

'I know what it is!' said he, slapping him on the shoulder.
'I, too, have been in your case! After I lost my poor dead wife
I used to go into the fields to be alone; I used to fall at the foot
of a tree, weep, call on the Good God, abuse him; I would
have wished to be like the moles I saw hanging on the
branches with maggots crawling in their bellies – dead, in a
word. And when I thought how other men at that very
moment were with their nice little wives, holding them in
their arms, I used to beat the ground with great blows of my
stick; I was pretty well mad; I hardly ate; the mere idea of
going to the cafe disgusted me, you would not believe. Ah,
well, very gradually, one day following another, spring on
winter and autumn on summer, all that passed away bit by
bit, little by little. It is gone, it has left me, sunk, I should
rather say, for there is still something deep down as who
should say . . . a weight, there, about the chest. But, since it

74

is the lot of us all, neither ought we to allow ourselves to repine, and because others are dead, wish to die ourselves . . . You must shake yourself up, M. Bovary; all that will pass! Come to see us; my daughter thinks of you now and then, remember, and she says that you are forgetting her. We shall have spring here directly; we will have you shoot a rabbit at the warren by way of a little distraction.'

Not long afterwards, Charles Bovary marries Rouault's daughter, Emma. After the wedding feast, the old man sees the couple off.

When he had taken about a hundred strides he stopped, and, as he watched the conveyance pass into the distance, with its wheels throwing up the dust, he heaved a deep sigh. Then he called to mind his own wedding, the old days, his wife's first pregnancy. He, also, had been very happy the day that he had led her from her father's house to his own, when he carried her on the crupper of his saddle as they trotted over the snow; for it was about Christmas time, and the country was all white. She had held him by one arm, having her basket slung on the other; the wind blew hither and thither the long pieces of lace employed in the dressing of her hair after the fashion of Caux. Sometimes they would fly across and touch his mouth, and when he turned his head he saw close to him, on his shoulder, her little rosy face, smiling silently beneath the golden badge on her bonnet. To warm her fingers she would thrust them from time to time into his bosom. How old and far away it was, all that! Their son would have been thirty now! Then he looked behind him; he could see nothing on the road. He felt sad as a house stripped of its furniture; and, tender remembrances mingling with dark thoughts in his brain muddled by the fumes of the junketing, for a moment he was conscious of a lively desire to go take a stroll by the church. As he feared, however, that the sight of it might make him still sadder, he went straight back home.

C. S. LEWIS

from *A Grief Observed*

And no one ever told me about the laziness of grief. Except at my job – where the machine seems to run on much as usual – I loathe the slightest effort. Not only writing but even reading a letter is too much. Even shaving. What does it matter now whether my cheek is rough or smooth? They say an unhappy man wants distractions – something to take him out of himself. Only as a dog-tired man wants an extra blanket on a cold night; he'd rather lie there shivering than get up and find one. It's easy to see why the lonely become untidy; finally, dirty and disgusting.

It is incredible how much happiness, even how much gaiety, we sometimes had together after all hope was gone. How long, how tranquilly, how nourishingly, we talked together that last night!

And yet, not quite together. There's a limit to the 'one flesh'. You can't really share someone else's weakness, or fear or pain. What you feel may be bad. It might conceivably be as bad as what the other felt, though I should distrust anyone who claimed that it was. But it would still be quite different. When I speak of fear, I mean the merely animal fear, the recoil of the organism from its destruction; the smothery feeling; the sense of being a rat in a trap. It can't be transferred. The mind can sympathise; the body, less. In one way the bodies of lovers can do it least. All their love passages have trained them to have, not identical, but complementary, correlative, even opposite, feelings about one another.

We both knew this. I had my miseries, not hers; she had hers, not mine.

I have no photograph of her that's any good. I cannot even see her face distinctly in my imagination. Yet the odd face of some stranger seen in a crowd this morning may come before me in vivid perfection the moment I close my eyes tonight. No doubt, the explanation is simple enough. We have seen the faces of those we know best so variously, from so many angles, in so many lights, with so many expressions – waking, sleeping, laughing, crying, eating, talking, thinking – that all the impressions crowd into our memory together and cancel out in a mere blur. But her voice is still vivid . . .

Already, less than a month after her death, I can feel the slow, insidious beginning of a process that will make the H. I think of into a more and more imaginary woman . . .

The reality is no longer there to check me, to pull me up short, as the real H. so often did, so unexpectedly, by being so thoroughly herself and not me.

Slowly, quietly, like snow-flakes – like the small flakes that come when it is going to snow all night – little flakes of me, my impressions, my selections, are settling down on the image of her. The real shape will be quite hidden in the end. Ten minutes – ten seconds – of the real H. would correct all this. And yet, even if those ten seconds were allowed me, one second later the little flakes would begin to fall again. The rough, sharp, cleansing tang of her otherness is gone.

What pitiable cant to say 'She will live forever in my memory!' *Live?* That is exactly what she won't do. You might as well think like the old Egyptians that you can keep the dead by embalming them.

I can't settle down. I yawn, I fidget, I smoke too much. Up till this I always had too little time. Now there is nothing but time. Almost pure time, empty successiveness.

One flesh. Or, if you prefer, one ship. The starboard engine has gone. I, the port engine, must chug along somehow till we make harbour. Or rather, till the journey ends.

I think there is also a confusion. We don't really want grief, in its first agonies, to be prolonged: nobody could. But we want something else of which grief is a frequent symptom, and then we confuse the symptom with the thing itself. I wrote the other night that bereavement is not the truncation of married love but one of its regular phases – like the honeymoon. What we want is to live our marriage well and faithfully through that phase too. If it hurts (and it certainly will) we accept the pains as a necessary part of this phase. We don't want to escape them at the price of desertion or divorce. Killing the dead a second time. We were one flesh. Now that it has been cut in two, we don't want to pretend that it is whole and complete. We will be still married, still in love. Therefore we shall still ache. But we are not at all – if we understand ourselves – seeking the aches for their own sake. The less of them the better, so long as the marriage is preserved. And the more joy there can be in the marriage between dead and living, the better.

The better in every way. For, as I have discovered, passionate grief does not link us with the dead but cuts us off from them. This becomes clearer and clearer. It is just at those moments when I feel least sorrow – getting into my

79

morning bath is usually one of them – that H. rushes upon my mind in her full reality, her otherness.

For in grief nothing 'stays put'. One keeps on emerging from a phase, but it always recurs. Round and round. Everything repeats. Am I going in circles, or dare I hope I am on a spiral?

But if a spiral, am I going up or down it?

Sorrow, however, turns out to be not a state but a process. It needs not a map but a history . . .

Grief is like a long valley, a winding valley where any bend may reveal a totally new landscape. As I've already noted, not every bend does. Sometimes the surprise is the opposite one; you are presented with exactly the same sort of country you thought you had left behind miles ago. That is when you wonder whether the valley isn't a circular trench. But it isn't. There are partial recurrences, but the sequence doesn't repeat.

It's not true that I'm always thinking of H. Work and conversation make that impossible. But the times when I'm not are perhaps my worst. For then, though I have forgotten the reason, there is spread over everything a vague sense of wrongness, of something amiss. Like in those dreams where nothing terrible occurs – nothing that would sound even remarkable if you told it at breakfast-time – but the atmosphere, the taste, of the whole thing is deadly. So with this. I see the rowan berries reddening and don't know for a moment why they, of all things, should be depressing. I hear a clock strike and some quality it always had before has gone out of the sound. What's wrong with the world to make it so flat, shabby, worn-out looking? Then I remember.

Something quite unexpected has happened. It came this morning early. For various reasons, not in themselves at all mysterious, my heart was lighter than it had been for many weeks. For one thing, I suppose I am recovering physically from a good deal of mere exhaustion . . . .

And suddenly at the very moment when, so far, I mourned H. least, I remembered her best. Indeed it was something (almost) better than memory; an instantaneous, unanswerable impression. To say it was like a meeting would be going too far. Yet there was that in it which tempts one to use those words. It was as if the lifting of the sorrow removed a barrier.

If, as I can't help suspecting, the dead also feel the pains of separation (and this may be one of their purgatorial sufferings), then for both lovers, and for all pairs of lovers without exception, bereavement is a universal and integral part of our experience of love. It follows marriage as normally as marriage follows courtship or as autumn follows summer. It is not a truncation of the process but one of its phases; not the interruption of the dance, but the next figure.

PART THREE

The Wear and Tear of Married Life

INTRODUCTION

♥

This part consists of marriages that (for better or worse) continue.

The opening two chapters of *Pride and Prejudice* illustrate most clearly the consequences for an intelligent man of marrying a pretty, silly woman. He is resigned to it, as people had to be in those days, and takes perverse pleasure in her inability to understand him. But he has the sense, when he has done teasing her, to comply with her wishes, no doubt because with five daughters he can also see the advantage of knowing an eligible young man.

I have included the Duke and Duchess of Hamilton because husbands buying finery for their spouses and almost infallibly making the wrong choice is a timeless problem, as all shops know after Christmas when ritzy, daring nightdresses and underwear are returned by the dozen by disgruntled wives. In the seventeenth century this was not an option.

Tolstoy is marvellous at depicting marriage and family life, Count Nicholas and Mary being only one illustration. Remarque's account of the Polish soldier being helped by his mates to enjoy his wife, whom he has not seen for two years, when she visits him in hospital must have seemed sensational when it was first published. It is written with a kind of freshness and simplicity that makes it very moving.

There are three extracts from Daniel Deronda, showing

the disastrous marriage between Gwendolen and Grandcourt. We are looking at marriage when the husband had absolute power; nineteenth-century novelists were well aware of the dangers that lurked once the eager, lively, young girl was entrapped by marriage. (Jonas Chuzzlewit and poor little Mercy Pecksniff is another example. Jonas was a nasty, evil sot, but Eliot's Grandcourt is fully equipped for the most ingenious cruelty).

Finally, there is a breakfast scene between Tony and Brenda Last where Waugh, with casual brilliance, prepares us for what is to come.

SYDNEY SMITH

A Definition of Marriage

My definition of marriage: . . . it resembles a pair of shears,
so joined that they cannot be separated; often moving in
opposite directions, yet always punishing anyone who
comes between them.

JANE AUSTEN

from *Pride and Prejudice*

It is a truth universally acknowledged, that a single man in possession of a good fortune must be in want of a wife.

However little known the feeling or views of such a man may be on his first entering a neighbourhood, this truth is so well fixed in the minds of the surrounding families, that he is considered as the rightful property of some one or other of their daughters.

'My dear Mr Bennett,' said his lady to him one day, 'have you heard that Netherfield Park is let at last?'

Mr Bennett replied that he had not.

'But it is,' returned she; 'for Mrs Long has just been here, and she told me all about it.'

Mr Bennett made no answer.

'Do not you want to know who has taken it?' cried his wife, impatiently.

'*You* want to tell me, and I have no objection to hearing it.'

This was invitation enough.

'Why, my dear, you must know, Mrs Long says that Netherfield is taken by a young man of large fortune from the north of England; that he came down on Monday in a chaise and four to see the place, and was so much delighted with it that he agreed with Mr Morris immediately; that he is to take possession before Michaelmas, and some of his servants are to be in the house by the end of next week.'

'What is his name?'

'Bingley.'

'Is he married or single?'

'Oh, single, my dear, to be sure! A single man of large fortune; four or five thousand a year. What a fine thing for our girls!'

'How so? how can it affect them?'

'My dear Mr Bennett,' replied his wife, 'how can you be so tiresome? You must know that I am thinking of his marrying one of them.'

'Is that his design in settling here?'

'Design? nonsense, how can you talk so! But it is very likely that he *may* fall in love with one of them, and therefore you must visit him as soon as he comes.'

'I see no occasion for that. You and the girls may go, or you may send them by themselves, which perhaps will be still better, for, as you are as handsome as any of them, Mr Bingley might like you the best of the party.'

'My dear, you flatter me. I certainly *have* had my share of beauty, but I do not pretend to be anything extraordinary now. When a woman has five grown-up daughters, she ought to give over thinking of her own beauty.'

'In such cases, a woman has not often much beauty to think of.'

'But, my dear, you must indeed go and see Mr Bingley when he comes into the neighbourhood.'

'It is more than I engage for, I assure you.'

'But consider your daughters. Only think what an establishment it would be for one of them. Sir William and Lady Lucas are determined to go, merely on that account; for in general, you know, they visit no newcomers. Indeed you must go, for it will be impossible for *us* to visit him, if you do not.'

'You are over scrupulous, surely. I daresay Mr Bingley will be very glad to see you; and I will send a few lines by you to assure him of my hearty consent to his marrying whichever he chooses of the girls; though I must throw in a good word for my little Lizzy.'

'I desire you will do no such thing. Lizzy is not a bit better than the others; and I am sure she is not half so handsome as Jane, nor half so good-humoured as Lydia. But you are always giving *her* the preference.'

'They have none of them much to recommend them,' replied he: 'they are all silly and ignorant like other girls; but Lizzy has something more of quickness than her sisters.'

'Mr Bennett, how can you abuse your own children in such a way? You take delight in vexing me. You have no compassion on my poor nerves.'

'You mistake me, my dear. I have a high respect for your nerves. They are my old friends. I have heard you mention them with consideration these twenty years at least.'

'Ah, you do not know what I suffer.'

'But I hope you will get over it, and live to see many young men of four thousand a year come into the neighbourhood.'

'It will be of no use to us, if twenty such should come, since you will not visit them.'

'Depend upon it, my dear, that when there are twenty, I will visit them all.'

Mr Bennett was so odd a mixture of quick parts, sarcastic humour, reserve, and caprice, that the experience of three-and-twenty years had been insufficient to make his wife understand his character. *Her* mind was less difficult to develop. She was a woman of mean understanding, little information, and uncertain temper. When she was discontented, she fancied herself nervous. The business of her life was to get her daughters married: its solace was visiting and news.

*

89

[Chapter Two] . . . Mr Bennett was among the earliest of those who waited on Mr Bingley. He had always intended to visit him, though to the last always assuring his wife that he should not go; and till the evening after the visit was paid she had no knowledge of it. It was then disclosed in the following manner. Observing his second daughter employed in trimming a hat, he suddenly addressed her with,

'I hope Mr Bingley will like it, Lizzy.'

'We are not in a way to know *what* Mr Bingley likes,' said her mother, resentfully, 'since we are not to visit.'

'But you forget, mamma,' said Elizabeth, 'that we shall meet him at the assemblies, and that Mrs Long has promised to introduce him.'

'I do not believe Mrs Long will do any such thing. She has two nieces of her own. She is a selfish, hypocritical woman, and I have no opinion of her.'

'No more have I,' said Mr Bennett; 'and I am glad to find that you do not depend on her serving you.'

Mrs Bennett deigned not to make any reply; but unable to contain herself, began scolding one of her daughters.

'Don't keep coughing so, Kitty, for heaven's sake! Have a little compassion on my nerves. You tear them to pieces.'

'Kitty has no discretion in her coughs,' said her father; 'she times them ill.'

'I do not cough for my own amusement,' replied Kitty, fretfully. 'When is your next ball to be, Lizzy?'

'Tomorrow fortnight.'

'Ay, so it is,' cried her mother, 'and Mrs Long does not come back till the day before; so, it will be impossible for her to introduce him, for she will not know him herself.'

'Then, my dear, you may have the advantage of your friend, and introduce Mr Bingley to *her*.'

'Impossible, Mr Bennett, impossible, when I am not acquainted with him myself; how can you be so teasing?'

'I honour your circumspection. A fortnight's acquaintance

is certainly very little. One cannot know what a man really is by the end of a fortnight. But if we do not venture, somebody else will; and after all, Mrs Long and her nieces must stand their chance; and, therefore, as she will think it an act of kindness, if you decline the office, I will take it on myself.'

The girls stared at their father. Mrs Bennett said only, 'Nonsense, nonsense!'

'What can be the meaning of that emphatic exclamation?' cried he. 'Do you consider the forms of introduction, and the stress that is laid on them, as nonsense? I cannot quite agree with you *there*. What say you, Mary? for you are a young lady of deep reflection, I know, and read great books, and make extracts.'

Mary wished to say something sensible, but knew not how.

'While Mary is adjusting her ideas,' he continued, 'let us return to Mr Bingley.'

'I am sick of Mr Bingley,' cried his wife.

'I am sorry to hear *that*; but why did not you tell me so before? If I had known as much this morning, I certainly would not have called on him. It is very unlucky; but as I have actually paid the visit, we cannot escape the acquaintance now.'

The astonishment of the ladies was just what he wished; that of Mrs Bennett perhaps surpassing the rest; though when the first tumult of joy was over, she began to declare that it was what she had expected all the while.

'How good it was in you, my dear Mr Bennett. But I knew I should persuade you at last. I was sure you loved your girls too well to neglect such an acquaintance. Well, how pleased I am! and it is such a good joke, too, that you should have gone this morning, and never said a word about it till now.'

'Now, Kitty, you may cough as much as you choose,' said Mr Bennett; and, as he spoke, he left the room, fatigued with the raptures of his wife.

'What an excellent father you have, girls,' said she, when the door was shut. 'I do not know how you will ever make him amends for his kindness; or me either, for that matter. At our time of life, it is not so pleasant, I can tell you, to be making new acquaintance every day; but for your sakes we would do anything. Lydia, my love, though you *are* the youngest, I daresay Mr Bingley will dance with you at the next ball.'

'Oh,' said Lydia, stoutly, 'I am not afraid; for though I *am* the youngest, I'm the tallest.'

The rest of the evening was spent in conjecturing how soon he would return Mr Bennett's visit, and determining when they should ask him to dinner.

DUCHESS ANNE

A London Outfit

The Duke and Duchess now made Hamilton Palace their permanent home. Whatever the Duke's motives in marrying, he and his wife enjoyed from the start an affectionate working partnership, and early on he told her that 'when I see the ways of others and thinks on you, I cannot but acknowledge myself most happy in so virtuous a person.' The birth of a large family completed their domestic felicity. On 30 April 1657, exactly a year and a day after their wedding, their first daughter was born. She was named Mary, after both her grandmothers. Even greater was the rejoicing when a year later the Duchess gave birth to a son and heir, James Earl of Arran. After that, the children followed at regular intervals: William, Anna, Katherine, Charles, John, George, Susan, Margaret, another Anna, Basil and Archibald. Mary, the eldest, died when she was nine and both little girls called Anna died in infancy, but seven sons and three daughters were to survive to adult life.

For the most part, the Duchess was content to wear the gowns made for her by John Muirhead, but there were occasions which demanded something much more splendid, and then a London outfit was what was required. This presented something of a problem, for the Duchess went south but rarely. On those occasions when she did accompany the Duke to Court she took the opportunity of making a round of all the dressmakers, but such chances for personal shopping were infrequent and to a large extent she had to rely on the services of an intermediary. At first she employed Andrew Cole, a faithful servant of her father's, to make her purchases for her: he even bought her petticoats and stays, but once the Duke himself was going to London regularly she relied on him to do her shopping.

This method of purchase was not without its difficulties. With a heavy heart and bearing a note of his wife's measurements, the Duke would set off for the dressmaker's. There he was presented with a dazzling display of materials: great bales of scarlet satin, yard upon yard of purple silk, lengths of crimson mohair and emerald green wool, not to mention quantities of gold and silver lace, ribbons of every imaginable colour, rosettes, bows, flounces – and an interminable list of queries. Would the Duchess wish her gown to be made of this style or of that? Of what colour should the dress be made? What type of trimming would she prefer? Should the petticoat be of a matching or of a contrasting colour? Fumbling his way through a maze of feminine terminology, the Duke knew despair. Sometimes he was not even certain what sort of garment he was ordering. There was the regrettable occasion when he asked the dressmaker to make up a 'sallantine' and the fellow did not seem to know what he meant. David Crawford did not know, the assistants did not know and the other customers did not know. He had to retire defeated to his lodgings, where further questioning of the landlady and the maids met with as little success. At last he wrote home in a rage to the Duchess, declaring that 'your "sallantine" I neither know what it is you mean by it nor can I find anybody that knows what it is, so explain yourself by the next [letter].' The Duchess replied at once, pointing out somewhat tartly that he had misread her writing. As everyone knew, the word was 'palantine', that highly fashionable accessory, a furred scarf. None too pleased, the Duke placed the desired order but he was soon embroiled in further difficulties. 'I wish you had let me know the price of the yard of the stuff you desire I should get to be a petticoat and mantle to Miss Mary Dunbar [their ward,] and what I should bestow on a palantine for her, and the price of the yard of the silk galloon and colour, and what of the beads and ribbons to wear on the head is for her and what for you.'

Sometimes the Duke was able to enlist the help of a female relative, and sometimes the Duchess tried to give him fairly explicit instructions. In 1678, for instance, she told her husband to go to Mr Renne the tailor and order for her a mantle of 'very grave colours', a black gown and a dark coloured petticoat. She emphasised most particularly that the garments must be of sober hue, and no doubt felt that she had been sufficiently specific in her requests. This time the Duke should have no trouble.

On receiving her letter, her husband duly set off for Mr Renne's, and as usual was shown a glittering selection of all kinds of cloth. He inspected material, looked at trimmings, fingered lace and made his choice. He returned home well satisfied. Unfortunately, history does not record the reaction of the Duchess when, some months later, the precious trunk arrived from London. Opening it up, no doubt with a feeling of pleasurable anticipation, she lifted out the flannel bundles inside, unrolled them carefully, and was confronted with a scarlet satin petticoat trimmed with silver and gold lace, a coloured and flowered silk gown and a flowered gown trimmed with lace! She had reckoned without the Duke's personal tastes.

COUNT LEV NIKOLAEVICH TOLSTOY

❧

'I can't get a moment's peace'

Nicholas suddenly moved and cleared his throat. And at that moment little Andrew shouted from outside the door: 'Papa! Mamma's standing here!' Countess Mary turned pale with fright and made signs to the boy. He grew silent, and quiet ensued for a moment, terrible to Countess Mary. She knew how Nicholas disliked being waked. Then through the door she heard Nicholas clearing his throat again and stirring, and his voice said crossly:

'I can't get a moment's peace. Mary, is that you? Why did you bring him here?'

'I only came in to look, and did not notice . . . forgive me . . .'

Nicholas coughed and said no more. Countess Mary moved away from the door and took the boy back to the nursery. Five minutes later little black-eyed three-year-old Natásha, her father's pet, having learnt from her brother that papa was asleep and mamma was in the sitting-room, ran to her father unobserved by her mother. The dark-eyed little girl boldly opened the creaking door, went up to the sofa with energetic steps of her sturdy little legs, and having examined the position of her father, who was asleep with his back to her, rose on tip-toe and kissed the hand which lay under his head. Nicholas turned with a tender smile on his face.

'Natásha, Natásha!' came Countess Mary's frightened whisper from the door. 'Papa wants to sleep.'

'No, mamma, he doesn't want to sleep,' said little Natásha with conviction. 'He's laughing.'

Nicholas lowered his legs, rose, and took his daughter in his arms.

'Come in, Mary,' he said to his wife.

She went in and sat down by her husband.

'I did not notice him following me,' she said timidly. 'I just looked in.'

Holding his little girl with one arm, Nicholas glanced at his wife and, seeing her guilty expression, put his other arm round her and kissed her hair.

'May I kiss mamma?' he asked Natásha.

Natásha smiled bashfully.

'Again!' she commanded, pointing with a peremptory gesture to the spot where Nicholas had placed the kiss.

'I don't know why you think I am cross,' said Nicholas, replying to the question he knew was in his wife's mind.

'You have no idea how unhappy, how lonely, I feel when you are like that. It always seems to me . . .'

'Mary, don't talk nonsense. You ought to be ashamed of yourself!' he said gaily.

'It seems to me that you can't love me, that I am so plain . . . always . . . and now . . . in this cond . . .'

'Oh, how absurd you are! It is not beauty that endears, it's love that makes us see beauty. It is only Malvínas and women of that kind who are loved for their beauty. But do I love my wife? I don't love her, but . . . I don't know how to put it. Without you, or when something comes between us like this, I seem lost and can't do anything. Now do I love my finger? I don't love it, but just try to cut it off!'

'I'm not like that myself, but I understand. So you're not angry with me?'

'Awfully angry!' he said, smiling and getting up. And smoothing his hair he began to pace the room.

ERICH MARIA REMARQUE

from *All Quiet on the Western Front*

*The year is 1916, the narrator is twenty; he has been wounded
after two years in the trenches and is now recovering in hospital
where it has just occurred to him that his 'knowledge of life is
limited to death'.*

The oldest man in our room is Lewandowski. He is forty,
and has already lain ten months in the hospital with a
severe abdominal wound. Just in the last few weeks he has
improved sufficiently to be able to hobble about doubled up.

For some days past, he has been in great excitement. His
wife has written to him from the little home in Poland where
she lives, telling him that she has saved up enough money
to pay for the fare, and is coming to see him.

She is already on the way and may arrive any day.
Lewandowski has lost his appetite, he even gives away red
cabbage and sausage after he has had a couple of mouth-
fuls. He goes round the room perpetually with the letter.
Everyone has already read it a dozen times, the post-marks
have been examined heaven knows how often, the address
is hardly legible any longer for spots of grease and
thumb-marks, and in the end what is sure to happen,
happens: Lewandowski develops a fever, and has to go back
to bed.

He has not seen his wife for two years. In the meantime she has given birth to a child, whom she is bringing with her. But something else occupies Lewandowski's thoughts. He had hoped to get permission to go out when his old woman came; for obviously seeing is all very well, but when a man gets his wife again after such a long time, if at all possible, a man wants something else besides.

Lewandowski has discussed it all with us at great length; in the army there are no secrets about such things. And what's more, nobody finds anything objectionable in it. Those of us who are already able to go out have told him of a couple of very good spots in the town, parks and squares, where he would not be disturbed; one of us even knows of a little room.

But what is the use, there Lewandowski lies in bed with his troubles. Life holds no more joy for him if he has to forego this affair. We console him and promise to get over the difficulty somehow or other.

One afternoon his wife appears, a tousled little thing with anxious, quick eyes like a bird, in a sort of black, crinkly mantilla with ribbons; heaven knows where she inherited the thing.

She murmurs something softly and stands shyly in the doorway. It terrifies her that there are six of us men present.

'Well, Marja,' says Lewandowski, and gulps dangerously with his Adam's apple, 'you can come in all right, they won't hurt you.'

She goes the round and proffers each of us her hand. Then she produces the child, which in the interval has done something in its napkin. From a large handbag embroidered with pearls she takes out a clean one and makes the child fresh and presentable. This dispels her first embarrassment, and the two begin to talk.

Lewandowski is very fidgety, every now and then he squints across at us most unhappily with his round goggle eyes.

The time is favourable, the doctor's visit is over, at the most there couldn't be more than one sister left in the ward. So one of us goes out to prospect. He comes back and nods.

'Not a soul to be seen. Now's your chance, Johann, set to.'

The two speak together in an undertone. The woman turns a little red and looks embarrassed. We grin good-naturedly and make pooh-poohing gestures, what does it matter! The devil take all the conventions, they were made for other times; here lies the carpenter Johann Lewandowski, a soldier shot to a cripple, and there is his wife; who knows when he will see her again? He wants to have her and he should have her, good.

Two men stand at the door to forestall the sisters and keep them occupied if they chance to come along. They agree to stand guard for a quarter of an hour or thereabouts.

Lewandowski can only lie on his side, so one of us props a couple of pillows against his back. Albert gets the child to hold, we all turn round a bit, the black mantilla disappears under the bed-clothes, we make a great clatter and play skat noisily.

All goes well. I hold a club solo with four jacks which nearly goes the round. In the process we almost forget Lewandowski. After a while the child begins to squall, although Albert, in desperation, rocks it to and fro. Then there is a bit of creaking and rustling, and as we look up casually we see that the child has the bottle in its mouth, and is back again with its mother. The business is over.

We now feel ourselves like one big family, the woman is rather quieter, and Lewandowski lies there sweating and beaming.

He unpacks the embroidered handbag, and a couple of good sausages come to light; Lewandowski takes up the knife with a flourish and saws the meat into slices.

With a handsome gesture he waves toward us – and the little woman goes from one to the other and smiles at us and hands round the sausage; she now looks quite handsome. We call her Mother, she is pleased and shakes up our pillows for us.

GEORGE ELIOT

❦

from *Daniel Deronda*

On the day when Gwendolen Harleth was married and became Mrs Grandcourt, the morning was clear and bright, and while the sun was low a slight frost crisped the leaves. The bridal party was worth seeing, and half Pennicote turned out to see it, lining the pathway up to the church. An old friend of the Rector's performed the marriage ceremony, the Rector himself acting as father, to the great advantage of the procession. Only two faces, it was remarked, showed signs of sadness – Mrs Davilow's and Anna's. The mother's delicate eyelids were pink, as if she had been crying half the night; and no one was surprised that, splendid as the match was, she should feel the parting from a daughter who was the flower of her children and of her own life. It was less understood why Anna should be troubled when she was being so well set off by the bridesmaid's dress. Every one else seemed to reflect the brilliancy of the occasion – the bride most of all. Of her it was agreed that as to figure and carriage she was worthy to be a 'lady o' title': as to face, perhaps it might be thought that a title required something more rosy; but the bridegroom himself not being fresh-coloured – being indeed, as the miller's wife observed, very much of her own husband's complexion – the match was the more complete. Anyhow he must be very fond of her;

and it was to be hoped that he would never cast it up to her that she had been going out to service as a governess, and her mother to live at Sawyer's Cottage – vicissitudes which had been much spoken of in the village. The miller's daughter of fourteen could not believe that high gentry behaved badly to their wives, but her mother instructed her – 'Oh, child, men's men: gentle or simple, they're much of a muchness. I've heard my mother say Squire Pelton used to take his dogs and a long whip into his wife's room, and flog 'em there to frighten her; and my mother was lady's-maid there at the very time.'

'That's unlucky talk for a wedding, Mrs Girdle,' said the tailor. 'A quarrel may end wi' the whip, but it begins wi' the tongue, and it's the women have got the most o' that.'

'The Lord gave it 'em to use, I suppose,' said Mrs Girdle; '*He* never meant you to have it all your own way.'

'By what I can make out from the gentleman as attends to the grooming at Offendene,' said the tailor, 'this Mr Grandcourt has wonderful little tongue. Everything must be done dummy-like without his ordering.'

'Then he's the more whip, I doubt,' said Mrs Girdle. '*She's* got tongue enough, I warrant her. See, there they come out together!'

'What wonderful long corners she's got to her eyes!' said the tailor. 'She makes you feel comical when she looks at you.'

. . . And Gwendolen was not without her after-thoughts that her husband's eyes might have been on her, extracting something to reprove – some offence against her dignity as his wife; her consciousness telling her that she had not kept up the perfect air of equability in public which was her own idea. But Grandcourt made no observation on her behaviour. All he said as they were driving home was –

103

'Lush will dine with us among the other people to-morrow. You will treat him civilly.'

Gwendolen's heart began to beat violently. The words that she wanted to utter, as one wants to return a blow, were, 'You are breaking your promise to me – the first promise you made me.' But she dared not utter them. She was as frightened at a quarrel as if she had foreseen that it would end with throttling fingers on her neck. After a pause, she said in the tone rather of defeat than resentment –

'I thought you did not intend him to frequent the house again.'

'I want him just now. He is useful to me; and he must be treated civilly.'

Silence. There may come a moment when even an excellent husband who had dropt smoking under more or less of a pledge during courtship, for the first time will introduce his cigar-smoke between himself and his wife, with the tacit understanding that she will have to put up with it. Mr Lush was, so to speak, a very large cigar.

If these are the sort of lovers' vows at which Jove laughs, he must have a merry time of it.

. . . No movement of Gwendolen in relation to Deronda escaped him [Grandcourt]. He would have denied that he was jealous; because jealousy would have implied some doubt of his own power to hinder what he had determined against. That his wife should have more inclination to another man's society than to his own would not pain him: what he required was that she should be as fully aware as she would have been of a locked hand-cuff, that her inclination was helpless to decide anything in contradiction with his resolve. However much of vacillating whim there might have been in his entrance on matrimony, there was no vacillating in his interpretation of the bond. He had not

104

repented of his marriage; it had really brought more of aim into his life, new objects to exert his will upon; and he had not repented of his choice. His taste was fastidious, and Gwendolen satisfied it: he would not have liked a wife who had not received some elevation of rank from him; nor one whose nails were not of the right shape; nor one the lobe of whose ear was at all too large and red; nor one who, even if her nails and ears were right, was at the same time a ninny, unable to make spirited answers. These requirements may not seem too exacting to refined contemporaries whose own ability to fall in love has been held in suspense for lack of indispensable details; but fewer perhaps may follow him in his contentment that his wife should be in a temper which would dispose her to fly out if she dared, and that she should have been urged into marrying him by other feelings than passionate attachment. Still, for those who prefer command to love, one does not see why the habit of mind should change precisely at the point of matrimony.

. . . But one morning when they were breakfasting, Gwendolen, in a recurrent fit of determination to exercise her old spirit, said, dallying prettily over her prawns without eating them –

'I think of making myself accomplished while we are in town, and having singing lessons.'

'Why?' said Grandcourt, languidly.

'Why?' echoed Gwendolen, playing at sauciness; 'because I can't eat *pâté de foie gras* to make me sleepy, and I can't smoke, and I can't go to the club to make me like to come away again – I want a variety of *ennui*. What would be the most convenient time, when you are busy with your lawyers and people, for me to have lessons from that little Jewess, whose singing is getting all the rage?'

'Whenever you like,' said Grandcourt, pushing away his plate, and leaning back in his chair while he looked at her with his most lizard-like expression, and played with the ears of the tiny spaniel on his lap (Gwendolen had taken a dislike to the dogs because they fawned on him).

Then he said, languidly, 'I don't see why a lady should sing. Amateurs make fools of themselves. A lady can't risk herself in that way in company. And one doesn't want to hear squalling in private.'

'I like frankness: that seems to me a husband's great charm,' said Gwendolen, with her little upward movement of her chin, as she turned her eyes away from his, and lifting a prawn before her, looked at the boiled ingenuousness of its eyes as preferable to the lizard's. 'But,' she added, having devoured her mortification, 'I suppose you don't object to Miss Lapidoth's singing at our party on the 4th? I thought of engaging her. Lady Brakenshaw had her, you know; and the Raymonds, who are very particular about their music. And Mr Deronda, who is a musician himself, and a first-rate judge, says that there is no singing in such good taste as hers for a drawing-room. I think his opinion is an authority.'

She meant to sling a small stone at her husband in that way.

'It's very indecent of Deronda to go about praising that girl,' said Grandcourt, in a tone of indifference.

'Indecent!' exclaimed Gwendolen, reddening and looking at him again, overcome by startled wonder, and unable to reflect on the probable falsity of the phrase – 'to go about praising.'

'Yes; and especially when she is patronised by Lady Mallinger. He ought to hold his tongue about her. Men can see what is his relation to her.'

'Men who judge of others by themselves,' said Gwendolen, turning white after her redness, and immediately smitten with a dread of her own words.

'Of course. And a woman should take their judgment –

else she is likely to run her head into the wrong place,' said Grandcourt, conscious of using pincers on that white creature. 'I suppose you take Deronda for a saint.'

'Oh dear no!' said Gwendolen, summoning desperately her almost miraculous power of self-control, and speaking in a high hard tone. 'Only a little less of a monster.'

She rose, pushed her chair away without hurry, and walked out of the room with something like the care of a man who is afraid of showing that he has taken more wine than usual. She turned the keys inside her dressing-room doors, and sat down for some time looking as pale and quiet as when she was leaving the breakfast-room. Even in the moments after reading the poisonous letter she had hardly had more cruel sensations than now; for emotion was at the acute point, where it is not distinguishable from sensation.

from *A Handful of Dust*

All over England people were waking up, queasy and despondent. Tony lay for ten minutes very happily planning the renovation of his ceiling. Then he rang the bell.

'Has her ladyship been called yet?'

'About a quarter of an hour ago, sir.'

'Then I'll have breakfast in her room.'

He put on his dressing-gown and slippers and went through into Guinevere.

Brenda lay on the dais.

She had insisted on a modern bed. Her tray was beside her and the quilt was littered with envelopes, letters and the daily papers. Her head was propped against a very small blue pillow; clean of make-up her face was almost colourless, rose-pearl, scarcely deeper in tone than her arms and neck.

'Well?' said Tony.

'Kiss.'

He sat by the tray at the head of the bed; she leant forward to him (a nereid emerging from fathomless depths of clear water). She turned her lips away and rubbed against his cheek like a cat. It was a way she had.

'Anything interesting?'

He picked up some of the letters.

'No. Mama wants nanny to send John's measurements. She's knitting him something for Christmas. And the mayor wants me to open something next month. I needn't, need I?'

'I think you'd better, we haven't done anything for him for a long time.'

'Well, you must write the speech. I'm getting too old for the girlish one I used to give them all. And Angela says, will we stay for the New Year?'

'That's easy. Not on her life, we won't.'

'I guessed not . . . though it sounds an amusing party.'

'You go if you like. I can't possibly get away.'

'That's all right. I knew it would be "no" before I opened the letter.'

'Well, what sort of pleasure can there be in going all the way to Yorkshire in the middle of winter?'

'Darling, don't be cross. I know we aren't going. I'm not making a thing about it. I just thought it might be fun to eat someone else's food for a bit.'

Then Brenda's maid brought in the other tray. He had it put by the window seat, and began opening his letters. He looked out of the window. Only four of the six church towers were visible that morning. Presently he said, 'As a matter of fact I probably *can* manage to get away that weekend.'

'Darling, are you sure you wouldn't hate it?'

'I daresay not.'

While he ate his breakfast Brenda read to him from the papers. 'Reggie's been making another speech . . . There's such an extraordinary picture of Babe and Jock . . . a woman in America has had twins by two different husbands. Would you have thought that possible? . . . Two more chaps in gas ovens . . . a little girl has been strangled in a cemetery with a bootlace . . . that play we went to about a farm is coming off.' Then she read him the serial.

109

He lit his pipe. 'I don't believe you're listening. Why doesn't Sylvia want Rupert to get the letter?'

'Eh? Oh well, you see, she doesn't really trust Rupert.'

'I *knew* it. There's no such character as Rupert in the story. I shall never read to you again.'

'Well, to tell you the truth I was just thinking.'

'Oh?'

'I was thinking how delightful it is, that it's Saturday morning and we haven't got anyone coming over for the weekend.'

'Oh, you thought that?'

'Don't you?'

'Well, it sometimes seems to me rather pointless keeping up a house this size if we don't now and then ask some other people to stay in it.'

'*Pointless?* I can't think what you mean. I don't keep up this house to be a hostel for a lot of bores to come and gossip in. We've always lived here and I hope John will be able to keep it on after me. One has a duty towards one's employees, and towards the place too. It's a definite part of English life which would be a serious loss if . . .' Then Tony stopped short in his speech and looked at the bed. Brenda had turned on her face and only the top of her head appeared above the sheets.

'Oh, God,' she said into the pillow. 'What have I done?'

'I say, am I being pompous again?'

She turned sideways so that her nose and one eye emerged. 'Oh no, darling, not *pompous*. You wouldn't know how.'

'Sorry.'

Brenda sat up. 'And, please, I didn't mean it. I'm jolly glad too, that no one's coming.'

(These scenes of domestic playfulness had been more or less continuous in Tony and Brenda's life for seven years).

PART FOUR

The Rough

INTRODUCTION

Difficult, painful, unhappy marriage seems to bring out the best in many a novelist. It has always been easier to speak or write about incompatibility of one kind or another than to communicate exactly how and how much marriage partners are in perfect accord. We all have far less to say about happiness than we have about any of its opposites, and this is largely because happiness is self-evident; it seldom inspires the curiosity for detailed confidence in anyone else, whereas unhappiness (often also self-evident) engenders a desire to help, to comfort, to advise – even, if the recipient is lucky, to listen to their woes.

Here are three exerpts from George Eliot's *Middlemarch*: poor Mrs Bulstrode reckoning with her husband's disgrace, Mr Casaubon's views on marriage, and two scenes between Lydgate and his wife Rosamond – the most agonising scenes of marital life I can recall – in which Lydgate comes to understand whom he has married. In *The Humbler Creation* Pamela Hansford Johnson shows us the wretched vicar Maurice chained to the awful Libby and fully conscious of what she is from page one. Robert Graves's depiction of the nuptials of John Milton with his bride is lightened by how spirited he makes her. And Galsworthy shows the ultimate helplessness of Soames when Irene leaves him.

I have included a piece from Richard Aldington's *Death of*

a Hero because, savage though it is, it none the less pinpoints a great deal of the cant that went on about love and marriage in the last century to the detriment of both partners.

Finally there is the wonderful chapter from Elizabeth von Arnim's novel *Vera* after young Lucy has married the monstrous Wemyss – a brilliant portrait of a tyrant with his prey.

GEORGE BERNARD SHAW

from *Man and Superman*

Those who talk most about the blessings of marriage and
the constancy of its vows are the very people who declare
that if the chain were broken and the prisoners let free to
choose, the whole social fabric would fly asunder. You
cannot have the argument both ways. If the prisoner is
happy, why lock him in? If he is not, why pretend that he is?

JOHN MILTON

❥

from *The Doctrine and Discipline of Divorce*

God in the first ordaining of marriage taught us to what end he did it, in words expressly implying the apt and cheerful conversation of man with woman, to comfort and refresh him against the evil of solitary life, not mentioning the purpose of generation till afterwards, as being but a secondary end in dignity, though not in necessity.

ROBERT GRAVES

from *The Story of Mary Powell, Wife to Mr Milton*

The rolling and jauncing of the coach over so many miles of
hard road would have wearied me, even had the earlier part
of my day been spent in an easy and careless manner; but
now I was so worn out that, over-passing the stage of
drowsiness, I was again wakeful, somewhat hysterical and
with a headache that seemed like a sword thrust in behind
my eyes.

The bridal chamber was hung with garlands, and
scented heavily with vervain and southernwood and with
bowls of flowers – the damask-rose, the carnation, and the
double-clove gillyflower – and there was a silver tray set
beside the bed with a flagon of wine and glasses and a dish
of little caraway cakes upon it, and the first nectarines and
John apples of the year. The white satin coverlet was
sprinkled with gold-dust, that glinted and winked in the
light of seven fat wax candles set in a glassen candelabrum
over the foot of the bed. Zara and Ann, who had slept in the
coach, now performed their part of bridesmaids, unlacing
me and taking off my shoes and stockings and underlinen
and leaving me naked at last between the fine linen sheets;
after which they sang a little song and told my brother
Richard, a brideman, to go call my husband in to me. Then
they kissed me good night. There was nothing in Zara's

116

manner of which I could complain, for she stood in awe of my husband; and Ann was her own sweet, childish self.

Then my husband came in, who locked the door; and, the shutters being already bolted, there we were alone together.

When he had taken off his clothes he climbed into the bed with a Bible in his hand. He kissed me tenderly, and began to read me out a portion from the Canticles, where Solomon praises his mistress for her beauty, likening her belly to an heap of wheat, and her breasts to two young roes which are twins. Then he closed the book, after he had put a petal or two of the rose between the leaves, as a remembrance; and spoke very lover-like and sweetly to me, but in some foreign language, which sounded so uncouth that I believe it to have been the Syriac or the Aramaic. Then I must get out of bed again and kneel down beside him and give thanks to God for his Infinite Bounty that he had created us male and female, with a deal more which I repeated after him. When our Amen was said he lifted me back again between the sheets and caught me in his arms and trembled with a strong passion. When I said nothing, but lay numb and stark, he raised my head, saying, 'Ah, modest reluctancy – I admire you!' and presented a cup of wine to my lips. I sipped a little, but though I had resolved to please him, I could not catch the infection of his passion. He wooed me next with a pretty tale of his going to Italy in search of a bride: how one day while he was at Cambridge University he had walked out into the country beyond Grantchester, and being weary of much study had slept beneath a tree by the roadside. Passed two handsome young ladies in a coach, of whom one (the handsomer, as he learned afterwards from one who saw what was done) had fallen in love with him as he lay there. She wrote with a pencil on a little piece of paper, which she then thrust into his sleeping hand, a verse in the Italian language to the effect that if his closed eyes had slain her with their beauty, what would they not do when open?

He could not by diligent inquiry discover who this lady was and had gone into Italy to seek her blindly. However, he had not found her there, and now being wed to me he regretted her not.

How could I answer him but with 'Oh' and 'Ah' and 'Hum'? As he spoke he toyed delicately with the ringlets of my hair.

A great lassitude from the heavy fragrance of the herbs and flowers overcame me; and the wine sickened my stomach, and 'Oh, Husband,' I cried, 'my head splits! Will you not fetch me a little cool water on a handkerchief, from the bowl of flowers standing in the window, and tie it about my brow?'

When a dog greyhound and a spaniel bitch once began coupling in the backside of our house at Forest Hill, Trunco caught them in the act and souse! she flung a pailful of cold water over them, which cooled the bitch's rut in a trice; as for Jack the greyhound, he stood shivering in a foolish manner which made us all laugh, and then began to howl dolefully. It would be exceeding indecent to compare that event with this, yet my inopportune request for the moistened handkerchief was no less rude a shock to my husband's nature than Trunco's dousing had been to Jack and Blanche. He looked chapfallen and incredulous and knew not what to say. Presently, disengaging his arms from about my shoulders, he blurted out: 'A headache! By the body of Bacchus and the sweet milk of Venus, only hearken now to the phlematic and ungrateful wretch! Where any other would almost have swooned with the luxury of being wooed with poetry and wine and prayer and the scent of roses and holy verbenas, and not in wanton disport but in the holy and legitimate bond of marriage – instead this miserable clod mewls out that she has a headache and would have me lay a wetted rag upon her brow!'

'I meant not to offend you Husband,' said I faintly, 'but if you had a headache to match mine I dare undertake that you would not be so poetical as this nor so impassionate. If you truly love me, as you say, you will give me what I ask.'

He replied: 'Nay, Child, I love you too well to indulge or yield to you even in so pelting a caprice as this. I am your husband, not your simpering gallant for whom disdainfully you drop a glove and expect that he will stoop to recover it; nay, nor any slobbering water-spaniel to whom you cry "go fetch, Sirrah!" If you must have a moistened handkerchief for your brow, I give you leave to fetch it yourself!'

I wept a little, but for pain and resentment, not for self-pity; then rising from the bed, and holding my head that throbbed like a drum, I went tottering to the window and dipped my fingers in the bowl of water, and dabbled my brow with it. Then I took up a silk neckerchief lying upon a table and was for using that as a bandage, when he roared at me not to handle his clothes; so I stumbled naked around the room, seeking a kerchief of my own. Yet since Trunco had not been suffered to come with me (who would have laid my necessaries neatly in a drawer for the night), I could find nothing, and came miserably back to bed.

'I am not in general subject to the headache,' I said, wishing to placate my husband as he sat upright in the bed, glowering at me, 'except when there is a storm brewing, or because of the flowers. Tonight——'

'The flowers!' he interrupted. 'What a froward, drivelling flibbergib have I taken to my bosom? The night air is cool and mild, so that she dare not accuse the weather of causing her pretended headache; then must she complain of these perfect roses – blooms surpassing those of Rhodes and Sharon, and archaically consecrate to nuptial rites?'

'Nay, Husband,' said I, holding my temples tight in my hands, 'you misunderstand me. I spoke then of *the flowers*, meaning that the time of month with me——'

119

He leaped out of bed and cried: 'Oh, heavens! Is it possible? Can she be so ignorant and sluttish or unthinking as to play this trick upon me? Wife, did your mother never tell you that these *flowers* defile a man, and that a husband must, by the Law of God, separate himself from his wife while they are upon her?'

I protested: 'Nay, they are not yet upon me; for all that I said was——'

'I heard all what you said, you moon-heifer,' he answered roughly. 'You know as well as I, or better, that the headache is the warning herald of your monthly sickness, and that therefore before morning, while I slept, I might have been defiled.'

He was so petulant, impatient, and thwart and my head ached so sorely that I could not venture upon a further explication; yet I meant to say no more than that the weather and the time of the month were, in general, the causes of my headaches, but that tonight it was the rumbling and joggling of the coach that had caused it. Well, it was easier to let him believe for the present that he could not enjoy me because of the time of the month; and in the morning, I hoped, the headache would be gone and perhaps he would laugh with me at our cross-purposes when I told him my meaning. Meanwhile, he rolled out the truckle-bed from under the great bed and tossed a blanket or two upon it and bade me lie down there, which I did, while he lay propped on an elbow with his back turned to me and read a Greek book which he had with him. I complained that the candle-light hurt my eyes, but he paid no heed to my complaint and continued reading; so I drew a tress of my hair over, and presently fell asleep.

GEORGE ELIOT

from *Middlemarch*

Harriet Bulstrode has just heard that her husband has been involved in shady dealings, and now faces a public scandal.

She locked herself in her room. She needed time to get used to her maimed consciousness, her poor lopped life, before she could walk steadily to the place allotted her. A new searching light had fallen on her husband's character, and she could not judge him leniently: the twenty years in which she had believed in him and venerated him by virtue of his concealments came back with particulars that made them seem an odious deceit. He had married her with that bad past life hidden behind him, and she had no faith left to protest his innocence of the worst that was imputed to him. Her honest ostentatious nature made the sharing of a merited dishonour as bitter as it could be to any mortal.

But this imperfectly-taught woman, whose phrases and habits were an odd patchwork, had a loyal spirit within her. The man whose prosperity she had shared through nearly half a life, and who had unvaryingly cherished her – now that punishment had befallen him it was not possible to her in any sense to forsake him. There is a forsaking which still sits at the same board and lies on the same couch with the forsaken soul, withering it the more by unloving proximity.

She knew, when she locked her door, that she should unlock it ready to go down to her unhappy husband and espouse his sorrow, and say of his guilt, I will mourn and not reproach. But she needed time to gather up her strength; she needed to sob out her farewell to all the gladness and pride of her life. When she had resolved to go down, she prepared herself by some little acts which might seem mere folly to a hard onlooker; they were her way of expressing to all spectators visible or invisible that she had begun a new life in which she embraced humiliation. She took off all her ornaments and put on a plain black gown, and instead of wearing her much-adorned cap and large bows of hair, she brushed her hair down and put on a plain bonnet-cap, which made her look suddenly like an early Methodist.

Bulstrode, who knew that his wife had been out and had come in saying that she was not well, had spent the time in an agitation equal to hers. He had looked forward to her learning the truth from others, and had acquiesced in that probability, as something easier to him than any confession. But now that he imagined the moment of her knowledge come, he awaited the result in anguish. His daughters had been obliged to consent to leave him, and though he had allowed some food to be brought to him, he had not touched it. He felt himself perishing slowly in unpitied misery. Perhaps he should never see his wife's face with affection in it again. And if he turned to God there seemed to be no answer but the pressure of retribution.

It was eight o'clock in the evening before the door opened and his wife entered. He dared not look up at her. He sat with his eyes bent down, and as she went towards him she thought he looked smaller – he seemed so withered and shrunken. A movement of new compassion and old tenderness went through her like a wave, and putting one hand on his which rested on the arm of the chair, and the other on his shoulder, she said, solemnly but kindly –

'Look up, Nicholas.'

He raised his eyes with a little start and looked at her half amazed for a moment: her pale face, her changed, mourning dress, the trembling about her mouth, all said, 'I know'; and her hands and eyes rested gently on him. He burst out crying and they cried together, she sitting at his side. They could not yet speak to each other of the shame which she was bearing with him, or of the acts which had brought it down on them. His confession was silent, and her promise of faithfulness was silent. Open-minded as she was, she nevertheless shrank from the words which would have expressed their mutual consciousness, as she would have shrunk from flakes of fire. She could not say, 'How much is only slander and false suspicion?' and he did not say, 'I am innocent.'

... 'Tertius did not find fault with me, then?' said Rosamond, understanding now that Lydgate might have said anything to Mrs Casaubon, and that she certainly was different from other women. Perhaps there was a faint taste of jealousy in the question. A smile began to play over Dorothea's face as she said –

'No, indeed! How could you imagine it?' But here the door opened, and Lydgate entered.

'I am come back in my quality of doctor,' said he. 'After I went away, I was haunted by two pale faces: Mrs Casaubon looked as much in need of care as you, Rosy. And I thought that I had not done my duty in leaving you together; so when I had been to Coleman's I came home again. I noticed that you were walking, Mrs Casaubon, and the sky has changed – I think we may have rain. May I send some one to order your carriage to come for you?'

'Oh no! I am strong; I need the walk,' said Dorothea, rising with animation in her face. 'Mrs Lydgate and I have chatted a great deal, and it is time for me to go. I have always been accused of being immoderate and saying too much.'

She put out her hand to Rosamond, and they said an earnest, quiet goodbye without kiss or other show of effusion: there had been between them too much serious emotion for them to use the signs of it superficially.

As Lydgate took her to the door she said nothing of Rosamond, but told him of Mr Farebrother and the other friends who had listened with belief to his story.

When he came back to Rosamond, she had already thrown herself on the sofa, in resigned fatigue.

'Well, Rosy,' he said, standing over her, and touching her hair, 'what do you think of Mrs Casaubon now you have seen so much of her?'

'I think she must be better than any one,' said Rosamond, 'and she is very beautiful. If you go to talk to her so often, you will be more discontented with me than ever!'

Lydgate laughed at the 'so often'. 'But has she made you any less discontented with me?'

'I think she has,' said Rosamond, looking up in his face. 'How heavy your eyes are, Tertius – and do push your hair back.' He lifted up his large white hand to obey her, and felt thankful for this little mark of interest in him. Poor Rosamond's vagrant fancy had come back terribly scourged – meek enough to nestle under the old despised shelter. And the shelter was still there: Lydgate had accepted his narrowed lot with sad resignation. He had chosen this fragile creature, and had taken the burthen of her life upon his arms. He must walk as he could, carrying that burthen pitifully.

. . . One morning, some weeks after her arrival at Lowick, Dorothea – but why always Dorothea? Was her point of view the only possible one with regard to this marriage? I

124

protest against all our interest, all our effort at understanding being given to the young skins that look blooming in spite of trouble; for these too will get faded, and will know the older and more eating griefs which we are helping to neglect. In spite of the blinking eyes and white moles objectionable to Celia, and the want of muscular curve which was morally painful to Sir James, Mr Casaubon had an intense consciousness within him, and was spiritually a-hungered like the rest of us. He had done nothing exceptional in marrying – nothing but what society sanctions, and considers an occasion for wreaths and bouquets. It had occurred to him that he must not any longer defer his intention of matrimony, and he had reflected that in taking a wife, a man of good position should expect and carefully choose a blooming young lady – the younger the better, because more educable and submissive – of a rank equal to his own, of religious principles, virtuous disposition, and good understanding. On such a young lady he would make handsome settlements, and he would neglect no arrangement for her happiness: in return, he should receive family pleasures and leave behind him that copy of himself which seemed so urgently required of a man – to the sonneteers of the sixteenth century. Times had altered since then, and no sonneteer had insisted on Mr Casaubon's leaving a copy of himself; moreover, he had not yet succeeded in issuing copies of his mythological key; but he had always intended to acquit himself by marriage, and the sense that he was fast leaving the years behind him, that the world was getting dimmer and that he felt lonely, was a reason to him for losing no more time in overtaking domestic delights before they too were left behind by the years.

And when he had seen Dorothea he believed that he had found even more than he demanded: she might really be such a helpmate to him as would enable him to dispense with a hired secretary, an aid which Mr Casaubon had never yet employed and had a suspicious dread of. (Mr Casaubon was nervously conscious that he was expected to manifest a powerful mind.) Providence, in its kindness, had supplied him with the wife he needed. A wife, a modest young lady, with the purely appreciative, unambitious abilities of her sex, is sure to think her husband's mind powerful. Whether Providence had taken equal care of Miss Brooke in presenting her with Mr Casaubon was an idea which could hardly occur to him. Society never made the preposterous demand that a man should think as much about his own qualifications for making a charming girl happy as he thinks of hers for making himself happy. As if a man could choose not only his wife but his wife's husband! Or as if he were bound to provide charms for his posterity in his person! – When Dorothea accepted him with effusion, that was only natural; and Mr Casaubon believed that his happiness was going to begin.

He had not had much foretaste of happiness in his previous life. To know intense joy without a strong bodily frame, one must have an enthusiastic soul. Mr Casaubon had never had a strong bodily frame, and his soul was sensitive without being enthusiastic: it was too languid to thrill out of self-consciousness into passionate delight; it went on fluttering in the swampy ground where it was hatched, thinking of its wings and never flying. His experience was of that pitiable kind which shrinks from pity, and fears most of all that it should be known: it was that proud narrow sensitiveness which has not mass enough to spare for transformation into sympathy, and quivers thread-like in small currents of self-preoccupation or at best of an egoistic scrupulosity. And Mr Casaubon had many scruples: he was capable of a severe self-restraint; he was resolute in being a man of honour according to the code; he would be unimpeachable by any recognised opinion.

*

. . . When Rosamond had finished reading the letter she sat quite still, with her hands folded before her, restraining any show of her keen disappointment, and intrenching herself in quiet passivity under her husband's wrath. Lydgate paused in his movements, looked at her again, and said, with biting severity –

'Will this be enough to convince you of the harm you may do by secret meddling? Have you sense enough to recognise now your incompetence to judge and act for me – to interfere with your ignorance in affairs which it belongs to me to decide on?'

The words were hard; but this was not the first time that Lydgate had been frustrated by her. She did not look at him, and made no reply.

'I had nearly resolved on going to Quallingham. It would have cost me pain enough to do it, yet it might have been of some use. But it has been of no use for me to think of anything. You have always been counteracting me secretly. You delude me with a false assent, and then I am at the mercy of your devices. If you mean to resist every wish I express, say so and defy me. I shall at least know what I am doing then.'

It is a terrible moment in young lives when the closeness of love's bond has turned to this power of galling. In spite of Rosamond's self-control a tear fell silently and rolled over her lips. She still said nothing; but under that quietude was hidden an intense effect: she was in such entire disgust with her husband that she wished she had never seen him. Sir Godwin's rudeness towards her and utter want of feeling ranged him with Dover and all other creditors – disagreeable people who only thought of themselves, and did not mind how annoying they were to her. Even her father was unkind, and might have done more for them. In fact there was but one person in Rosamond's world whom she did not regard as blameworthy, and that was the graceful creature

127

with blond plaits and with little hands crossed before her, who had never expressed herself unbecomingly, and had always acted for the best – the best naturally being what she best liked.

Lydgate pausing and looking at her began to feel that half-maddening sense of helplessness which comes over passionate people when their passion is met by an innocent-looking silence whose meek victimised air seems to put them in the wrong, and at last infects even the justest indignation with a doubt of its justice. He needed to recover the full sense that he was in the right by moderating his words.

'Can you not see, Rosamond,' he began again, trying to be simply grave and not bitter, 'that nothing can be so fatal as a want of openness and confidence between us? It has happened again and again that I have expressed a decided wish, and you have seemed to assent, yet after that you have secretly disobeyed my wish. In that way I can never know what I have to trust to. There would be some hope for us if you would admit this. Am I such an unreasonable, furious brute? Why should you not be open with me?'

Still silence.

'Will you only say that you have been mistaken, and that I may depend on your not acting secretly in the future?' said Lydgate, urgently, but with something of request in his tone which Rosamond was quick to perceive. She spoke with coolness.

'I cannot possibly make admissions or promises in answer to such words as you have used towards me. I have not been accustomed to language of that kind. You have spoken of my "secret meddling", and my "interfering ignorance", and my "false assent". I have never expressed myself in that way to you, and I think that you ought to apologise. You spoke of its being impossible to live with me. Certainly you have not made my life pleasant to me of late. I think it was to be expected that I should try to avert some of the hardships which our marriage has brought on me.' Another tear fell as Rosamond ceased speaking, and she pressed it away as quietly as the first.

Lydgate flung himself into a chair, feeling checkmated. What place was there in her mind for a remonstrance to lodge in? He laid down his hat, flung an arm over the back of his chair, and looked down for some moments without speaking. Rosamond had the double purchase over him of insensibility to the point of justice in his reproach, and of sensibility to the undeniable hardships now present in her married life. Although her duplicity in the affair of the house had exceeded what he knew, and had really hindered the Plymdales from knowing of it, she had no consciousness that her action could rightly be called false. We are not obliged to identify our own acts according to a strict classification, any more than the materials of our grocery and clothes. Rosamond felt that she was aggrieved, and that this was what Lydgate had to recognise.

As for him, the need of accommodating himself to her nature, which was inflexible in proportion to its negations, held him as with pincers. He had begun to have an alarmed foresight of her irrevocable loss of love for him, and the consequent dreariness of their life. The ready fulness of his emotions made this dread alternate quickly with the first violent movements of his anger. It would assuredly have been a vain boast in him to say that he was her master.

'You have not made my life pleasant to me of late' – 'the hardships which our marriage has brought on me' – these words were stinging his imagination as a pain makes an exaggerated dream. If he were not only to sink from his highest resolve, but to sink into the hideous fettering of domestic hate?

'Rosamond,' he said, turning his eyes on her with a melancholy look, 'you should allow for a man's words

129

when he is disappointed and provoked. You and I cannot have opposite interests. I cannot part my happiness from yours. If I am angry with you, it is that you seem not to see how any concealment divides us. How could I wish to make anything hard to you either by my words or conduct? When I hurt you, I hurt part of my own life. I should never be angry with you if you would be quite open with me.'

'I have only wished to prevent you from hurrying us into wretchedness without any necessity,' said Rosamond, the tears coming again from a softened feeling now that her husband had softened. 'It is so very hard to be disgraced here among all the people we know, and to live in such a miserable way. I wish I had died with the baby.'

She spoke and wept with that gentleness which makes such words and tears omnipotent over a loving-hearted man. Lydgate drew his chair near to hers and pressed her delicate head against his cheek with his powerful tender hand. He only caressed her; he did not say anything; for what was there to say? He could not promise to shield her from the dreaded wretchedness, for he could see no sure means of doing so. When he left her to go out again, he told himself that it was ten times harder for her than for him: he had a life away from home, and constant appeals to his activity on behalf of others. He wished to excuse everything in her if he could – but it was inevitable that in that excusing mood he should think of her as if she were an animal of another and feebler species. Nevertheless she had mastered him.

JOHN GALSWORTHY

from *The Forsyte Saga*

Soames went upstairs that night with the feeling that he had gone too far. He was prepared to offer excuses for his words.

He turned out the gas still burning in the passage outside their room. Pausing, with his hand on the knob of the door, he tried to shape his apology, for he had no intention of letting her see that he was nervous.

But the door did not open, nor when he pulled it and turned the handle firmly. She must have locked it for some reason, and forgotten.

Entering his dressing-room, where the gas was also alight and burning low, he went quickly to the other door. That too was locked. Then he noticed that the camp bed which he occasionally used was prepared, and his sleeping- suit laid out upon it. He put his hand up to his forehead, and brought it away wet. It dawned on him that he was barred out.

He went back to the door, and rattling the handle stealthily, called: 'Unlock the door, do you hear? Unlock the door!'

There was a faint rustling, but no answer.

'Do you hear? Let me in at once – I insist on being let in!'

He could catch the sound of her breathing close to the door, like the breathing of a creature threatened by danger.

131

There was something terrifying in this inexorable silence, in the impossibility of getting at her. He went back to the other door, and putting his whole weight against it, tried to burst it open. The door was a new one – he had had them renewed himself, in readiness for their coming in after the honeymoon. In a rage he lifted his foot to kick in the panel; the thought of the servants restrained him, and he felt suddenly that he was beaten.

Flinging himself down in the dressing-room, he took up a book.

But instead of the print he seemed to see his wife – with her yellow hair flowing over her bare shoulders, and her great dark eyes – standing like an animal at bay. And the whole meaning of her act of revolt came to him. She meant it to be for good.

He could not sit still, and went to the door again. He could still hear her, and he called: 'Irene! Irene!'

He did not mean to make his voice pathetic. In ominous answer, the faint sounds ceased. He stood with clenched hands, thinking.

Presently he stole round on tiptoe, and running suddenly at the other door, made a supreme effort to break it open. It creaked, but did not yield. He sat down on the stairs and buried his face in his hands.

For a long time he sat there in the dark, the moon through the skylight above laying a pale smear that lengthened slowly towards him down the stairway. He tried to be philosophical.

Since she had locked her doors she had no further claim as a wife, and he would console himself with other women!

It was but a spectral journey he made among such delights – he had no appetite for these exploits. He had never had much, and he had lost the habit. He felt that he could never recover it. His hunger could only be appeased by his wife, inexorable and frightened, behind these shut doors. No other woman could help him.

This conviction came to him with terrible force out there in the dark.

His philosophy left him; and surly anger took its place. Her conduct was immoral, inexcusable, worthy of any punishment within his power. He desired no one but her, and she refused him!

She must really hate him, then! He had never believed it yet. He did not believe it now. It seemed to him incredible. He felt as though he had lost for ever his power of judgment. If she, so soft and yielding as he had always judged her, could take this decided step – what could not happen?

. . . Soames hastened home, oblivious; his hands trembled as he took the late letters from the gilt wire cage into which they had been thrust through the slit in the door.

None from Irene.

He went into the dining-room, the fire was bright there, his chair drawn up to it, slippers ready, spirit case, and carven cigarette box on the table; but after staring at it all for a minute or two, he turned out the light and went upstairs. There was a fire too in his dressing-room, but her room was dark and cold. It was into this room that Soames went.

He made a great illumination with candles, and for a long time continued pacing up and down between the bed and the door. He could not get used to the thought that she had really left him, and as though still searching for some message, some reason, some reading of all the mystery of his married life, he began opening every recess and drawer.

There were her dresses; he had always liked, indeed insisted, that she should be well-dressed – she had taken very few; two or three at most, and drawer after drawer, full of linen and silk things, was untouched.

Perhaps after all it was only a freak, and she had gone to the seaside for a few days' change. If only that were so, and she were really coming back, he would never again do as he had done that fatal night before last, never again run that risk – though it was her duty, her duty as a wife; though she did belong to him – he would never again run that risk; she was evidently not quite right in her head!

He stooped over the drawer where she kept her jewels; it was not locked and came open as he pulled; the jewel box had the key in it. This surprised him until he remembered that it was sure to be empty. He opened it.

It was far from empty. Divided, in little green velvet compartments, were all the things he had given her, even her watch, and stuck into the recess that contained the watch was a three-cornered note addressed 'Soames Forsyte', in Irene's handwriting.

'I think I have taken nothing that you or your people have given me.' And that was all.

He looked at the clasps and bracelets of diamonds and pearls, at the little flat gold watch with a great diamond set in sapphires, at the chains and rings, each in its nest, and the tears rushed up in his eyes and dropped upon them.

Nothing that she could have done, nothing that she *had* done, brought home to him like this the inner significance of her act. For the moment, perhaps, he understood nearly all there was to understand – understood that she loathed him, that she had loathed him for years, that for all intents and purposes they were like people living in different worlds, that there was no hope for him, never had been; even, that she had suffered – that she was to be pitied.

In that moment of emotion he betrayed the Forsyte in him – forgot himself, his interests, his property – was capable of almost anything; was lifted into the pure ether of the selfless and unpractical.

Such moments pass quickly.

And as though with the tears he had purged himself of weakness, he got up, locked the box, and slowly, almost trembling, carried it with him into the other room.

RICHARD ALDINGTON

❧

from *Death of a Hero*

Can one tabulate the ignorances, the relevant ignorances, of George Augustus and Isabel when they pledged themselves until death do us part?

George Augustus did not know how to make a living; he did not know in the very least how to treat a woman; he did not know how to live with a woman; he did not know how to make love to a woman – in fact, he was all minus there, for his experience with whores had been sordid, dismal and repulsive; he did not know the anatomy of his own body, let alone the anatomy of a woman's body; he did not know that pregnancy is a nine months' illness; he had not the least idea that childbirth costs money if the woman is not to suffer vilely; he did not know that a married man dependent on his and his wife's parents is an abject, helpless, and contemptible figure; he did not know that it is hard to earn a decent living even when you have 'a Profession'; he knew damn little about even his profession; he knew very little indeed about the conditions of life and nothing about human psychology; he knew nothing about business and about money, except how to spend it; he knew nothing about indoor sanitation, food values, carpentry, house-furnishing, shopping, fire-lighting, chimney-sweeping, higher mathematics, Greek, domestic invective, making the

136

worse appear the better cause, how to feed a baby, music, dancing, Swedish drill, opening sardine-tins, boiling eggs, which side of the bed to sleep with a woman, charades, gas stoves, and an infinity of other things all indispensable to a married man.

He must have been rather a dull dog.

As for Isabel – what she didn't know includes almost the whole range of human knowledge. The puzzle is to find out what she *did* know. She didn't even know how to buy her own clothes – Ma Hartly had always done that for her. Among the things she did not know were: how babies are made and come; how to make love; how to pretend she was enjoying it even when she wasn't; how to sew, wash, cook, scrub, run a house, purchase provisions, keep household accounts, domineer over a housemaid, order a dinner, dismiss a cook, know when a room was clean, manage George Augustus when he was in a bad temper, give George Augustus a pill when he was liverish, feed and wash a baby and pin on its napkins, pay and receive calls, knit, crochet, make pastry, how to tell a fresh herring is stale, the difference between pork and veal, never to use margarine, how to make a bed comfortably, look after her health especially in pregnancy, produce the soft answer which turneth away wrath, keep the home fires burning, and an infinity of other things indispensable to a married woman.

(I really wonder how poor old George managed to get born at all.)

On the other hand, both George Augustus and Isabel knew how to read and write, pray, eat, drink, wash themselves, and dress up on Sundays. They were both pretty well acquainted with the Bible and Hymns A. and M.

The honeymoon did not take place in Paris or on the Plains

137

of Waterloo, but in a South Coast watering-place, a sweetly pretty spot Isabel had always wanted to visit. They had a ten-mile drive from the village to the railway, and a two hours' journey in a train which stopped at every station. They arrived tired, shy, and disappointed at the small but respectable hotel where a double room had been booked.

The marriage night was a failure. One might *almost* have foreseen it. George Augustus tried to be passionate and ecstatic, and merely succeeded in being clumsy and brutal. Isabel tried to be modestly yielding and complying, and was only *gauche.* And, as many a sweet Victorian bride of dear old England in the golden days of Good Queen Vicky, she lay awake hour after hour, while George Augustus slept stertorously, thinking, thinking, while the tears ran out of her eyes, as she lay on her back, and trickled slowly down her temples on to the bridal pillow . . .

It's too painful, it's really too painful – all this damn silly 'purity' and cant and Luv and ignorance. And silly, ignorant girls handed over in their ignorance and sweetly-prettiness to ignorant and clumsy young men for them to brutalise and wound in their ignorance. It's too painful to think of. Poor Isabel! What an initiation!

But, of course, that ghastly night had its consequences. In the first place, it meant that the marriage was legally consummated, and could not be broken without an appeal to the Divorce Courts – and I don't even know if you could get divorced in the golden days of grand old Mr Gladstone, bless his heart, may hell be hot for him. And then it meant that Isabel shrank from sexual intercourse with George Augustus for the rest of her days; and, since she was a woman of considerable temperament, *that* implied the twenty-two lovers already stirring the womb of futurity. And finally, since Isabel was as healthy as a young woman

138

could be who had to wear madly tight corsets and long insanitary hair and long insanitary skirts, and who had rudimentary ideas of sex hygiene – finally, that *nuit de rêve* gave Isabel her first baby.

❦

from *The Humbler Creation*

Libby came in. She had washed her face, changed her suit for a dress. It was a new one, of some olive-green stuff, the top of it draped like a chiton. She stood against the fireplace, one arm disposed along the shelf. 'I bought it while we were away. Do you like it? I know we can't afford it. But I was tempted and fell.'

'Oh, I expect we can. It's very nice.'

'Come here.'

She raised both arms into the air, contemplated him, and allowed her hands to sink on to his shoulders. She was pushing her beauty at him again: he wished she would not do it in front of Kate, who always looked away and smiled at nothing. Whether it was a smile of contempt or a smile for lovers, he had never been sure. Certainly she always spoke as if she still thought they were lovers, but it was not always easy to match Kate's words to her thoughts.

'Now,' said Libby reasonably, with the calm air which gave such confidence to people who did not know her, 'I am well aware that I got into a state. But I did act for the best. Mother *might* have been really ill. And, when all's said and done, aren't you just a little glad to have me home again?'

He told her how glad he was.

'And of course to have me,' said Kate from the sideboard,

'and Mother, and the boys, mad as wet hens. So nice for you. I suspect you've been having a wonderful time on your own.'

'He's been lonely,' Libby said confidently, 'and he looks thin. We are simply never going to desert him again, not all of us at the same time, because he hates it, though he's been awfully unselfish in letting us go.'

She put her arm round his waist and swung him back and forth a little, as in some very decorous dance.

She looked so proud of discovering that everything had turned out for the best, that he was swept with tenderness for her. When Kate went out to the kitchen, he kissed her and told her once more how much he liked her dress.

'Oh, you're a dear!' She yawned. 'A dear, a dear. What should I do without you? Or,' she added with firm quaintness, 'you without me?' She paused, and yawned again. 'I'm dog-tired. And the boys will be beastly to me at supper. I do wish you'd talk to them. After all, they haven't got a father, and it *is* your place.'

'Kate doesn't think so,' said Maurice. 'They're not so bad.'

'No, I know. And after all, they are,' she added, with a nod, 'one's own flesh and blood.'

They went up early to bed. She undressed, as she always did, in the bathroom, and returned to brush her hair before the glass. She did this slowly, ritually, stroking rather than brushing, from the pale crown to the straight, darker ends, first over the left shoulder, then over the right: she never took her gaze from the gaze of her own reflected eyes. 'I know I have been silly,' she said at last, in a meek voice. 'I do get upset.'

She put down the brush. Head hanging, she sat there. Her hair was arranged now in plaits over her back. If she could have made it speak to him, it would have said, Look! look! look!

141

The faint hope revived. It was a long time since they had been parted for more than a night or so. She might even be feeling differently about him, after so much absence. He came to her and set his hand in the small of her back. She turned on it, as on a swivel, and looked up at him. There is something silly about Libby's face, he thought, and the shock of the thought made him drop his hand. He beat it down by spurring his own desire. He lifted her, almost roughly. 'Come to bed.'

'Well, of course,' she said, laughing like a good-natured, badgered housewife. 'Well, of course, of course! I told you, I was worn out!'

She dropped gracefully on to her knees in prayer. He hesitated, then knelt beside her, and when he had finished, waited patiently. Her prayers were always much longer than his. He knew that tonight she was praying as a defence against him (well, she needn't worry, she was safe now), and wondered, as often before, whether she had always prayed so. He was a sensual man: his body had been a nuisance to him. He had married Libby because she had seemed, beneath her smilingness and her calm, to match his own sensuality; for years he had, on the whole, believed this was true. Yet he had never made love to her with an innocent heart. As a boy, he had been frightened by his desires; as a student at Cambridge he had yielded to them for the first time, and had found he could be perfectly happy provided he pushed all thought of his vocation out of the way. Sex was too like sin to be comfortable. He had talked the problem over with older and wiser men, laymen and priests: had accepted intellectually all they said to him, but could not feel the reassurance in himself. When he married he could worship God and enjoy Libby: but not, somehow, do both at the same time. He was disconcerted when she had insisted that they should pray together before getting into bed. She was right, he knew, and he was wrong: all the same, it spoiled joy for him. She was smudging with – with what? – some kind of falsehood, of *theatricality*, something that could have been more innocent for him, laying less of a weight upon his conscience. She made him feel guilty – why, he did not know. No well-adjusted man, priest or no priest, should feel so with his own wife. He had felt worse when he realised one night that Libby's desires were faked. If she prayed, it was for the power to submit cheerfully. He was bitterly humiliated; humiliation crept like sour water under his tongue.

A year ago, her prayers in this respect had mysteriously ceased to be effective. Without the slightest warning, she had informed him solemnly one night that she thought she was 'past all that sort of thing'. It was physiological, she explained. It did sometimes happen to women early. She was very grave, sweet and reasonable. She recognised the strain she might put on him. 'But,' she said, 'you *are* forty-four. And you have enormous strength of character.'

For some time after that, he had found his strength of character hardly equal to her conviction; he had desired her, and he had taken her. She had behaved cheerfully. But slowly, without a further word or gesture, she had managed to discourage him.

. . . 'All right,' said Libby, 'say it.'

'I haven't anything to say.'

She was standing beside his chair. Putting out his arm he clasped her around the thighs and drew her to him. It was all he could do.

It was nearly midnight. She had just come in from the rehearsal, which he had left an hour before. The household had gone up to bed. There was no sound but the rush of water from an overflow pipe; Simon took baths at eccentric hours and Kate had long since given up trying to stop him.

143

'You see,' said Libby patiently, 'it is my time of life. You don't know anything about medicine, darling, you admit you don't. But I do know a bit. I've missed three times in the past year, and that is always the beginning. I know it's hard on you to be specially patient, but you do have to be. And I *am* patient with you. I'm not going to reproach you for butting in on the rehearsal, though you shouldn't have done it. I'm sure Plym didn't thank you for it, not really.'

He did not speak. He was going through a bad spell that week, and he knew he must keep a check on his tongue. After twelve months, the habit of continence still refused to come easily. For weeks it might be all right: and then, perhaps for three or four days at a stretch, he would find it almost intolerable. At such times he thought (trying to laugh away an ill as adhesive to his whole nature as a cancer) that he understood the temptation of Saint Anthony. It would begin with some innocent image: Libby and himself on Midsummer Common, one evening in Cambridge at the bluest hour of a warm evening, turning to kiss after a quarrel; a slack afternoon in Leeds before a winter fire, when she had stretched out, with firelight on her arms, to pick up beads from a broken necklace. But it would spark off the demon, he would be sick with love for the past, to make love to her not as she was now, but then. The hot rods of pain would begin to throb, in his loins, his spine, down from his shoulders; he could feel the vibration of desire in his wrists. And as there was nothing to be done for it, he would be racked with irritation; it was hard for him to speak gently to anyone with this misery caged inside him. A sharp word could be something of a release: an expression of an old grudge, spat out like a broken tooth, almost a complete check to the tumult. Yet he knew he did not dare to take this way out. At such times he believed he had no right to be a priest, and he was tempted to envy those without faith. For his was steady enough; he had always felt God, as he had said to old Imber, like heat or cold; but he had always known that at times it was impossible to reach him. God was there, all right, as a king might be inside a palace: but there was no way of breaching the walls to him, of making passage through the armies of court officials, the secretaries, equerries, chamberlains, whom Maurice had made in the image of his own sins and weaknesses.

'What you lack,' said Libby, 'is any capacity to understand how other people feel. It's called empathy, isn't it? You haven't got it. You're turning away from me because of something I can't help, something physiological.' She gave him a strained, brave stare: she was tense in his embrace.

'Look,' he said, 'we can't quarrel any more: the time for that has passed. Don't you see? We can't, because we can no longer make anything good of quarrelling. It can't end in the way it should if it isn't to go sour, not any longer.'

'Sex?' She snipped it off as she might have snipped a tape with scissors. He felt the quiver of her contempt.

'If you like.'

'It's not what I like, it's what you like.' Pulling away from him, she made a turn to the fireplace more dramatic and more graceful than anything she had been able to achieve for Plymmer. She faced him, beseeching, spreading her arms, somehow contriving to give the impression that she wore draperies, that her hair was flowing. 'Dear, I didn't mean that. Only, can't you be patient? You're not young, neither of us are – '

'Bosh,' said Maurice uncontrollably.

'Don't you dare!'

This time he apologised, and Libby said, 'It sounds mean of me to say it, I know, but . . . well, I should think so!'

'I can't say more.'

She said, 'You don't love me. You haven't for some time. I *know*,' and her face was innocent with misery.

145

He got up and cuddled her to him, rocked her to and fro; he was full of a remorse that was somehow like rage. 'I do. Of course I do.'

She told him he did not. He was miles away from her; he criticised her; he had spoken to her sharply in front of strangers.

'Tonight? Lib, I didn't!'

'I didn't mean tonight.'

'When, then?'

'Never mind.'

'But when? You must tell me!'

Exhausted, they fell into something that was like the silence of amity.

'Better go up,' he said. He started clearing up his desk and she helped him efficiently.

That night she offered herself to him. He tried to take her and failed.

Through her tired and muffled weeping, he could detect her satisfaction. Hadn't she been right, after all? She was convinced that his desire was on the decrease, that soon everything would be all right, the way she wished it to be, without any crudity, indignity, or silliness.

He knew he would never touch her again.

ELIZABETH VON ARNIM

❦

from *Vera*

Marriage, Lucy found, was different from what she had supposed; Everard was different. For one thing she was always sleepy. For another she was never alone. She hadn't realised how completely she would never be alone, or, if alone, not sure for one minute to the other of going on being alone. Always in her life there had been intervals during which she recuperated in solitude from any strain; now there were none. Always there had been places she could go to and rest in quietly, safe from interruption; now there were none. The very sight of their room at the hotels they stayed at, with Wemyss's suit-cases and clothes piled on the chairs, and the table covered with his brushes and shaving things – for he wouldn't have a dressing-room, being too natural and wholesome, he explained, to want anything separate from his own woman – the very sight of this room fatigued her. After a day of churches, pictures and restaur-ants – he was a most conscientious sightseer, besides being greatly interested in his meals – to come back to this room wasn't rest but further fatigue. Wemyss, who was never tired and slept wonderfully – it was the soundness of his sleep that kept her awake, because she wasn't used to hearing sound sleep so close – would fling himself into the one easy-chair and pull her on to his knee, and having

147

kissed her a great many times he would ruffle her hair, and then when it was all on ends like a boy's coming out of a bath look at her with the pride of possession and say, 'There's a wife for a respectable British business man to have! Mrs Wemyss, aren't you ashamed of yourself?' And then there would be more kissing – jovial, gluttonous kisses, that made her skin rough and chapped.

'Baby,' she would say, feebly struggling, and smiling a little wearily.

Yes, he was a baby, a dear, high-spirited baby, but a baby now at very close quarters and one that went on all the time. You couldn't put him in a cot and give him a bottle and say, 'There now,' and then sit down quietly to a little sewing; you didn't have Sundays out; you were never, day or night, an instant off duty. Lucy couldn't count the number of times a day she had to answer the question, 'Who's my own little wife?' At first she answered it with laughing ecstasy, running into his outstretched arms, but very soon that fatal sleepiness set in and remained with her for the whole of her honeymoon, and she really felt too tired sometimes to get the ecstasy she quickly got to know was expected of her into her voice. She loved him, she was indeed his own little wife, but constantly to answer this and questions like it satisfactorily was a great exertion. Yet if there was a shadow of hesitation before she answered, a hair's-breath of delay owing to her thoughts having momentarily wandered, Wemyss was upset, and she had to spend quite a long time reassuring him with the fondest whispers and caresses. Her thoughts mustn't wander, she had discovered; her thoughts were to be his as well as all the rest of her. Was ever a girl so much loved? she asked herself, astonished and proud; but, on the other hand, she was dreadfully sleepy.

Any thinking she did had to be done at night, when she lay awake because of the immense emphasis with which

Wemyss slept, and she hadn't been married a week before she was reflecting what a bad arrangement it was, the way ecstasy seemed to have no staying power. Also it oughtn't to begin, she considered, at its topmost height and accordingly not be able to move except downwards. If one could only start modestly in marriage with very little of it and work steadily upwards, taking one's time, knowing there was more and more to come, it would be much better, she thought. No doubt it would go on longer if one slept better and hadn't, consequently, got headaches. Everard's ecstasy went on. Perhaps by ecstasy she really meant high spirits, and Everard was beside himself with high spirits.

Wemyss was indeed the typical bridegroom of the Psalms, issuing forth rejoicing from his chamber. Lucy wished she could issue forth from it rejoicing too. She was vexed with herself for being so stupidly sleepy, for not being able to get used to the noise beside her at night and go to sleep as naturally as she did in Eaton Terrace, in spite of the horns of taxis. It wasn't fair to Everard, she felt, not to find a wife in the morning matching him in spirits. Perhaps, however, this was a condition peculiar to honeymoons, and marriage, once the honeymoon was over, would be a more tranquil state. Things would settle down when they were back in England, to a different, more separated life in which there would be time to rest, time to think; time to remember, while he was away at his office, how deeply she loved him. And surely she would learn to sleep; and once she slept properly she would be able to answer his loving questions throughout the day with more real *élan*.

But – there in England waiting for her, inevitable, no longer to be put off or avoided, was The Willows. Whenever her thoughts reached that house they gave a little jump and tried to slink away. She was ashamed of herself, it was ridiculous, and Everard's attitude was plainly the sensible one, and if he could adopt it surely she, who hadn't gone through that terrible afternoon last July, could; yet she failed to see herself in The Willows, she failed altogether to imagine it. How, for instance, was she going to sit on that terrace – 'We always have tea in fine weather on the terrace,' Wemyss had casually remarked, apparently quite untouched by the least memory – how was she going to have tea on the very flags perhaps where . . . ? Her thoughts slunk away; but not before one of them had sent a curdling whisper through her mind, '*The tea would taste of blood.*'

Well, this was sleeplessness. She never in her life had had that sort of absurd thought. It was just that she didn't sleep, and so her brain was relaxed and let the reins of her thinking go slack. The day her father died, it's true, when it began to be evening and she was afraid of the night alone with him in his mysterious indifference, she had begun thinking absurdly, but Everard had come and saved her. He could save her from this too if she could tell him; only she couldn't tell him. How could she spoil his joy in his home? It was the thing he loved next best to her.

As the honeymoon went on and Wemyss's ecstasies a little subsided, as he began to tire of so many trains – after Paris they did the chateaux country – and hotels and waiters and taxis and restaurants, and the cooking which he had at first enjoyed now only increased his longing at every meal for a plain English steak and boiled potatoes, he talked more and more of The Willows. With almost the same eagerness as that which had so much enchanted and moved her before their marriage when he talked of their wedding day, he now talked of The Willows and the day when he would show it to her. He counted the days now to that day. The 4th of April; his birthday; on that happy day he would lead his little wife into the home he loved. How could she, when he talked like that, do anything but pretend enthusiasm and looking forward? He had apparently entirely forgotten what she had told him about her reluctance to go there at Christmas. She was astonished that, when the first bliss of being married to her had worn off and his thoughts were free for this other thing he so much loved, his home, he didn't approach it with more care for what he must know was her feeling about it. It would be, she felt, impossible to shadow his happiness at the prospect of showing her his home by any reminder of her reluctance. Besides, she was certainly going to have to live at The Willows, so what was the use of talking?

'I suppose,' she did say hesitatingly one day when he was describing it to her for the hundredth time, for it was his habit to describe the same thing often, 'you've changed your room——?'

They were sitting at the moment, resting after the climb up, on one of the terraces of the Chateau of Amboise, with a view across the Loire of an immense horizon, and Wemyss had been comparing it, to its disadvantage, when he recovered his breath, with the view from his bedroom window at The Willows. It wasn't very nice weather, and they both were cold and tired, and it was still only eleven o'clock in the morning.

'Changed my room? What room?' he asked.

'Your—— the room you and—— the room you slept in.'

'My bedroom? I should think not. It's the best room in the house. Why do you think I've changed it?' And he looked at her with a surprised face.

'Oh, I don't know,' said Lucy, taking refuge in stroking his hand. 'I only thought——'

An inkling of what was in her mind penetrated into his, and his voice went grave.

'You mustn't think,' he said. 'You mustn't be morbid. Now Lucy, I can't have that. It will spoil everything if you

151

let yourself be morbid. And you promised me before our marriage you wouldn't be. Have you forgotten?'

He turned to her and took her face in both his hands and searched her eyes with his own very solemn ones, while the woman who was conducting them over the castle went to the low parapet, and stood with her back to them studying the view and yawning.

'Oh, Everard – of course I haven't forgotten. I've not forgotten anything I promised you, and never will. But – have I got to go into that bedroom too?'

He was really astonished. 'Have you got to go into that bedroom too?' he repeated, staring at the face enclosed in his two big hands. It looked extraordinarily pretty like that, very like a small flower in its delicate whiteness next to his discoloured, middle-aged hands, and her mouth since her marriage seemed to have become an even more vivid red than it used to be, and her eyes were young enough to be made more beautiful instead of less by the languor of want of sleep. 'Well, I should think so. Aren't you my wife?'

'Yes,' said Lucy. 'But——'

'Now, Lucy, I'll have no buts,' he said, with his most serious air, kissing her on the cheek – she had discovered that just that kind of kiss was a rebuke. 'Those buts of yours butt in——'

He stopped, struck by what he had said.

'I think that was rather amusing – don't you?' he asked, suddenly smiling.

'Oh yes – very,' said Lucy eagerly, smiling too, delighted that he should switch off from solemnity.

He kissed her again, this time a real kiss, on her funny, charming mouth.

'I suppose you'll admit,' he said, laughing and squeezing up her face into a quaint crumpled shape, 'that either you're my wife or not my wife, and that if you're my wife——'

'Oh, I'm *that* all right,' laughed Lucy.

'Then you share my room. None of these damned new-fangled notions for me, young woman.'

'Oh, but I didn't mean——'

'What? Another but?' he exclaimed, pouncing down on to her mouth and stopping it with an enormous kiss.

'*Monsieur et Madame se refroidiront*,' said the woman, turning round and drawing her shawl closer over her chest as a gust of chilly wind swept over the terrace.

They were honeymooners, poor creatures, and therefore one had patience; but even honeymooners oughtn't to wish to embrace in a cold wind on an exposed terrace of a chateau round which they were being conducted by a woman who was in a hurry to return to the preparation of her Sunday dinner. For such purposes hotels were provided, and the shelter of a comfortable warm room. She had supposed them to be *père et fille* when first she admitted them, but was soon aware of their real relationship. '*Il doit être bien riche,*' had been her conclusion.

'Come along, come along,' said Wemyss, getting up quickly, for he too felt the gust of cold wind. 'Let's finish the chateau or we'll be late for lunch. I wish they hadn't preserved so many of these places – one would have been quite enough to show us the sort of thing.'

'But we needn't go and look at them all,' said Lucy.

'Oh yes we must. We've arranged to.'

'But Everard——' began Lucy, following after him as he followed after the conductress, who had a way of darting out of sight round corners.

'This woman's like a lizard,' panted Wemyss, arriving round a corner only to see her disappear through an arch. 'Won't we be happy when it's time to go back to England and not have to see any more sights?'

'But why don't we go back now, if you feel like it?' asked Lucy, trotting after him as he on his big legs pursued the retreating conductress, and anxious to show him, by eagerness to go sooner to The Willows than was arranged, that she wasn't being morbid.

'Why, you know we can't leave before the 3rd of April,' said Wemyss, over his shoulder. 'It's all settled.'

'But can't it be unsettled?'

'What, and upset all the plans, and arrive home before my birthday?' He stopped and turned round to stare at her. 'Really, my dear——' he said.

She had discovered that my dear was a term of rebuke.

'Oh yes – of course,' she said hastily, 'I forgot about your birthday.'

At that Wemyss stared at her harder than ever; incredulously, in fact. Forgot about his birthday? *Lucy* had forgotten? If it had been Vera, now – but Lucy? He was deeply hurt. He was so much hurt that he stood quite still, and the conductress was obliged, on discovering that she was no longer being followed, to wait once more for the honeymooners; which she did, clutching her shawl round her abundant French chest and shivering.

What had she said, Lucy hurriedly asked herself, running over her last words in her mind, for she had learned by now what he looked like when he was hurt. Oh yes – the birthday. How stupid of her. But it was because birthdays in her family were so unimportant, and nobody had minded whether they were remembered or not.

'I didn't mean that,' she said earnestly, laying her hand on his breast. 'Of course I hadn't forgotten anything so precious. It only had – well, you know what even the most wonderful things do sometimes – it – it had escaped my memory.'

'Lucy! Escaped your memory? The day to which you owe your husband?'

Wemyss said this with such an exaggerated solemnity, such an immense pomposity, that she thought he was in fun and hadn't really minded about the birthday at all; and,

154

eager to meet every mood of his, she laughed. Relieved, she was so unfortunate as to laugh merrily.

To her consternation, after a moment's further stare he turned his back on her without a word and walked on.

Then she realised what she had done, that she had laughed – oh, how dreadful! – in the wrong place, and she ran after him and put her arm through his, and tried to lay her cheek against his sleeve, which was difficult because of the way their paces didn't match and also because he took no notice of her, and said, 'Baby – baby – were his dear feelings hurt then?' and coaxed him.

But he wouldn't be coaxed. She had wounded him too deeply – laughing, he said to himself, at what was to him the most sacred thing in life, the fact that he was her husband, that she was his wife.

'Oh, Everard,' she murmured at last, withdrawing her arm, giving up, 'don't spoil our day.'

Spoil their day? He? That finished it.

He didn't speak to her again till night. Then, in bed, after she had cried bitterly for a long while, because she couldn't make out what really had happened, and she loved him so much, and wouldn't hurt him for the world, and was heartbroken because she had, and anyhow was tired out, he at last turned to her and took her to his arms again and forgave her.

'I can't live,' sobbed Lucy, 'I can't live – if you don't go on loving me – if we don't understand——'

'My little Love,' said Wemyss, melted by the way her small body was shaking in his arms, and rather frightened, too, at the excess of her woe. 'My little Love – don't. You mustn't. Your Everard loves you, and you mustn't give way like this. You'll be ill. Think how miserable you'd make him then.'

And in the dark he kissed away her tears, and held her close till her sobbing quieted down; and presently, held

155

close like that, his kisses shutting her smarting eyes, she now the baby comforted and reassured, and he the soothing nurse, she fell asleep, and for the first time since her marriage slept all night.

PART FIVE

The Best of It

INTRODUCTION

❧

The last part of this anthology shows above all the inestim-
able comforts and joys of a good marriage: a partnership
like no other. The tributes here of wife to husband, husband
to wife are all illuminating about the particular nature of
the relationship. There is not one way to be happily
married, although there are factors that many have in
common: respect, for instance – of the kind that comes from
a good working equality – none of the patronising praise
from men or breathless sentiment from women. Richard
Aldington would be amazed at the comfort and reality that
a natural balance of power can bring to chronic intimacy.

We begin with three statements from Luther, Disraeli and
James Thurber that speak for themselves.

William Ogilvie was the tutor to Emily Lennox's children
when she was married to the Duke of Leinster. By the time
the Duke died, they had been lovers for some time and he
married her after about a year of her widowhood. The
marriage was entirely happy: here is Ogilvie writing to her
after forty-five years.

Jane Austen did not often write about successful marriage, but Admiral and Mrs Croft from *Persuasion* are a
beautiful example.

Samuel Bishop sounds an ideal husband. A poem and a
ring – what more could one ask?

Serious loving is not always painless. Helen Thomas

writes very touchingly about her marriage to the poet Edward Thomas.

The Fuciks are a heroic example of love. Reading about them reminded me of the old couple on the *Titanic*, who I believe were called Strauss. Mrs Strauss was being conducted to one of the lifeboats, but when she realised that her husband was not included, turned back, took his arm and went to sit on a bench with him to wait for the ship to go down.

This part ends on an autumnal note: Darwin about his wife, Admiral Collingwood in a letter to his wife, Prevost and finally Shakespeare, capturing different essences of enduring love.

BENJAMIN DISRAELI

❦

from a letter to Princess Louise on
her engagement, 1870

There is no greater risk, perhaps, than matrimony, but there is nothing happier than a happy marriage.

JAMES THURBER

What is Love?

A lady of forty-seven who has been married twenty-seven years and has six children knows what love really is and once described it for me like this: 'Love is what you've been through with someone.'

,

Ogilvie to Emily Lennox

Ogilvie nurtured their love through the winter of Emily's old age, coaxing it gently as if they were still young and she would never die. He still sent her love letters when he went away; in August 1812 he wrote from Dublin,

> I last night after dinner received your letter of the 6th written as beautifully and with as steady a hand as the first letter I had the happiness of receiving from you about forty-five years ago. How can I ever be sufficiently thankful to Providence for continuing the blessing of my life to me, and with a degree of health and strength that enable you to bear up against the infirmities of old age and to enjoy the different objects that attach you to life, or how can I ever be sufficiently grateful to you dearest Emily for the steadiness and warmth of your attachment to me. Be assured, my beloved Emily that I am thoroughly sensible of and properly grateful for the one and the other . . . I can truly assure you that from the first moment of our attachment to this instant you have been the first and reigning object of my thought and feeling and that you will continue to be so till the last hour of my life and that no other object has ever engaged my affections or interfered with my attachment to you.

Ogilvie, at seventy, still acted like a young man,

planning, investing, travelling and building. He assumed that Emily could maintain her youthfulness too. For a long time she did. In 1811 Sarah described her as 'in wonderful health for 80'. She still dined out, visited her children and went to nursery gardens for plants ('to the detriment of my pocket'). Her grandson 'little Eddy' who had lived with her since Lord Edward Fitzgerald's death, absorbed much of her attention when he arrived home from Eton in the holidays. Emily watched her grandchildren's political development carefully. While Fox was alive she had taken 'little Eddy' on ritual visits to St Anne's Hill. After Fox's death, when his mantle passed to the third Lord Holland, Emily looked to Holland House for guidance. In 1808 she asked Lord Holland for help in sending the young Duke of Leinster, just out of Eton, some suitable Foxite reading. 'You would I trust, help to form, steady and fix his principles in the political way particularly; you can't imagine how much I have this at heart!'

Gradually time took its toll. In 1813 Emily suddenly grew old. 'Little Eddy' embarked for the Peninsula in February and his departure left her low and 'not well'. She revived in the summer. Ogilvie thought her well enough for him to go to Ireland for several weeks, from where he sent a last, loving note on 16 July. It ended, 'God bless you, I am your most tenderly affectionate husband WO.' But from then on, Emily's 'constitution of iron', as she called it, steadily failed. In the spring of 1814 she had a bout of pneumonia, from which she seemed to recover. 'Thank God the attack is over,' wrote her daughter Cecilia. 'She has thrown off an illness which would have killed anyone but herself. When I came yesterday they thought she had not two hours to live, but today she is well. Pulse calm, head quiet, heat gone.' But Emily's invincibility was only imagined by a family which she had dominated majestically for so long. In the third week of March illness returned, and on the

27 March she died. She was eighty-two years old, a woman who had had two husbands, twenty-two children and many secrets.

JANE AUSTEN

❧

from *Persuasion*

The Admiral, after taking two or three refreshing turns about the room with his hands behind him, being called to order by his wife, now came up to Captain Wentworth, and without any observation of what he might be interrupting, thinking only of his own thoughts, began with –

'If you had been a week later at Lisbon, last spring, Frederick, you would have been asked to give a passage to Lady Mary Grierson and her daughters.'

'Should I? I am glad I was not a week later then.'

The Admiral abused him for his want of gallantry. He defended himself; though professing that he would never willingly admit any ladies on board a ship of his, excepting for a ball or a visit, which a few hours might comprehend.

'But, if I know myself,' said he, 'this is from no want of gallantry towards them. It is rather from feeling how impossible it is, with all one's efforts, and all one's sacrifices, to make the accommodations on board such as women ought to have. There can be no want of gallantry, Admiral, in rating the claims of women to every personal comfort *high* – and this is what I do. I hate to hear of women on board, or to see them on board; and no ship, under my command, shall ever convey a family of ladies anywhere, if I can help it.'

This brought his sister upon him.

'Oh, Frederick! But I cannot believe it of you. All idle refinement! Women may be as comfortable on board as in the best house in England. I believe I have lived as much on board as most women, and I know nothing superior to the accommodations of a man-of-war. I declare I have not a comfort or an indulgence about me, even at Kellynch Hall,' with a kind bow to Anne, 'beyond what I always had in most of the ships I have lived in; and they have been five altogether.'

'Nothing to the purpose,' replied her brother. 'You were living with your husband; and were the only woman on board.'

'But you yourself brought Mrs Harville, her sister, her cousin, and the three children round from Portsmouth to Plymouth. Where was this superfine, extraordinary sort of gallantry of yours, then?'

'All merged in my friendship, Sophia. I would assist any brother officer's wife that I could, and I would bring anything to Harville's from the world's end, if he wanted it. But do not imagine that I did not feel it an evil in itself.'

'Depend upon it, they were all perfectly comfortable.'

'I might not like them the better for that, perhaps. Such a number of women and children have no *right* to be comfortable on board.'

'My dear Frederick, you are talking quite idly. Pray, what would become of us poor sailors' wives, who often want to be conveyed to one port or another, after our husbands, if everybody had your feelings?'

'My feelings, you see, did not prevent my taking Mrs Harville, and all her family, to Plymouth.'

'But I hate to hear you talking so, like a fine gentleman, and as if women were all fine ladies, instead of rational creatures. We none of us expect to be in smooth water all our days.'

'Ah, my dear,' said the Admiral, 'when he has got a wife, he will sing a different tune. When he is married, if we have the good luck to live to another war, we shall see him do as you and I, and a great many others, have done. We shall have him very thankful to anybody that will bring him his wife.'

'Ay, that we shall.'

'Now I have done,' cried Captain Wentworth. 'When once married people begin to attack me with – "Oh, you will think very differently when you are married," I can only say, "No, I shall not;" and then they say again, "Yes, you will," and there is an end of it.'

He got up and moved away.

'What a great traveller you must have been, ma'am!' said Mrs Musgrove to Mrs Croft.

'Pretty well, ma'am, in the fifteen years of my marriage; though many women have done more. I have crossed the Atlantic four times, and have been once to the East Indies, and back again, and only once; besides being in different places about home – Cork, and Lisbon, and Gibraltar. But I never went beyond the Streights, and never was in the West Indies. We do not call Bermuda or Bahama, you know, the West Indies.'

Mrs Musgrove had not a word to say in dissent; she could not accuse herself of having ever called them anything in the whole course of her life.

'And I do assure you, ma'am,' pursued Mrs Croft, 'that nothing can exceed the accommodations of a man-of-war; I speak, you know, of the higher rates. When you come to a frigate, of course, you are more confined; though any reasonable woman may be perfectly happy on one of them; and I can safely say, that the happiest part of my life has been spent on board a ship. While we were together, you know, there was nothing to be feared. Thank God! I have always been blessed with excellent health, and no climate disagrees with me. A little disordered always the first twenty-four hours of going to sea, but never knew what sickness was afterwards. The only time that I ever really suffered in body or mind, the only time that I ever fancied myself unwell, or had any ideas of danger, was the winter that I passed by myself at Deal, when the Admiral (*Captain* Croft then) was in the North Seas. I lived in perpetual fright at that time, and had all manner of imaginary complaints from not knowing what to do with myself, or when I should hear from him next; but as long as we could be together, nothing ever ailed me, and I never met with the smallest inconvenience.'

'Ay, to be sure. Yes, indeed, oh yes, I am quite of your opinion, Mrs Croft,' was Mrs Musgrove's hearty answer. 'There is nothing so bad as a separation. I am quite of your opinion. *I* know what it is, for Mr Musgrove always attends the assizes, and I am so glad when they are over, and he is safe back again.'

SAMUEL BISHOP

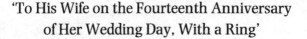

'To His Wife on the Fourteenth Anniversary of Her Wedding Day, With a Ring'

'Thee, Mary, with this ring I wed,'
So, fourteen years ago, I said.
Behold another ring! 'For what?'
To wed thee o'er again – why not?

With that first ring I married youth,
Grace, beauty, innocence, and truth;
Taste long admired, sense long revered,
And all my Molly then appeared.

If she, by merit since disclosed,
Prove twice the woman I supposed,
I plead that double merit now,
To justify a double vow.

Here then, to-day, – with faith as sure,
With ardour as intense and pure,
As when amidst the rites divine
I took thy troth, and plighted mine, –
To thee, sweet girl, my second ring,
A token, and a pledge, I bring;

With this I wed, till death us part,
Thy riper virtues to my heart;
Those virtues which, before untried,
The wife has added to the bride –
Those virtues, whose progressive claim,
Endearing wedlock's very name,
My soul enjoys, my song approves,
For conscience' sake as well as love's.

For why? – They show me every hour
Honour's high thought, affection's power,
Discretion's deed, sound judgment's sentence,
And teach me all things – but repentance.

HELEN THOMAS

♥

from *World Without End*

My love for him never lost its passionate intensity. My letters to him were love-letters, and his home coming meant for me to be lifted into Heaven.

We cannot say why we love people. There is no reason for passionate love. But the quality in him that I most admired was his sincerity. There was never any pretence between us. All was open and true. Often he was bitter and cruel, but I could bear it because I knew all. There was nothing left for me to guess at, no lies, no falsity. All was known, all was suffered and endured; and afterwards there was no reserve in our joy. If we love deeply we must also suffer deeply; for the price for the capacity for ecstatic joy is anguish. And so it was with us to the end.

JULIUS FUCIK

❦

Prison Notes

Julius Fucik, a journalist, was born in Prague on 23 February 1903 and was among the leaders of the Communist resistance movement in Czechoslovakia. He was arrested by the Gestapo on 24 April 1942 and executed on 8 September 1943. Notes he made during his imprisonment were found subsequently, among which was this:

It was during the period of martial law. The middle of June of last year. She was seeing me for the first time since our arrest, after six weeks of suffering spent in solitude in her cell, brooding over reports that announced my death. They called her in to soften me up.

'Talk to him,' the division chief said to her on confronting her with me. 'Urge him to be reasonable. If he won't think of himself, he might at least think of you. You have an hour to think it over. If he is still obdurate after that, you will be shot tonight. Both of you.'

She caressed me with her glance and answered simply: 'Officer, that's no threat for me, that's my last wish: If you are going to kill him, kill me too.'

CHARLES DARWIN

To His Sons

You all know your mother, and what a good mother she has ever been to all of you. She has been my greatest blessing and I can declare that in my whole life I have never heard her utter one word which I would rather have been unsaid. She has never failed in kindest sympathy towards me, and has borne with the utmost patience my frequent complaints of ill-health and discomfort. I do not believe she has ever missed an opportunity of doing a kind action to anyone near her. I marvel at my good fortune, that she, so infinitely my superior in every single moral quality, consented to be my wife. She has been my wise adviser and cheerful comforter throughout life, which without her would have been during a very long period a miserable one from ill-health. She has earned the love and admiration of every soul near her.

ADMIRAL LORD COLLINGWOOD

❧

Letter to his wife, 1806

Ocean, 16 June 1806

This day, my love, is the anniversary of our marriage, and I wish you many happy returns of it. If ever we have peace, I hope to spend my latter days amid my family, which is the only sort of happiness I can enjoy. After this life of labour to retire to peace and quietness is all I look for in the world. Should we decide to change the place of our dwelling, our route would of course be to the southward of Morpeth; but then I should be for ever regretting those beautiful views which are nowhere to be exceeded; and even the rattling of that old waggon that used to pass our door at six o'clock in a winter's morning had its charms. The fact is, whenever I think how I am to be happy again, my thoughts carry me back to Morpeth, where, out of the fuss and parade of the world, surrounded by those I loved most dearly, and who loved me, I enjoyed as much happiness as my nature is capable of. Many things that I see in the world give me a distaste to the finery of it. The great knaves are not like those poor unfortunates, who, driven perhaps to distress from accidents which they could not prevent, or at least not educated in principles of honour and honesty, are hanged for some little thievery; while a knave of education and

174

high-breeding, who brandishes his honour in the eyes of the world, would rob a state to its ruin. For the first I feel pity and compassion; for the latter, abhorrence and contempt; they are the tenfold vicious.

Have you read – but what I am more interested about, is your sister with you, and is she well and happy? Tell her – God bless her! – I wish I were with you, that we might have a good laugh. God bless me! I have scarcely laughed these three years. I am here with a very reduced force, having been obliged to make detachments to all quarters. This leaves me weak, while the Spaniards and French within are daily gaining strength. They have patched and pieced until they have now a very considerable fleet. Whether they will venture out, I do not know; if they come, I have no doubt we shall do an excellent deed, and then I will bring them to England myself.

How do the dear girls go on? I would have them taught geometry, which is of all sciences in the world the most entertaining; it expands the mind more to the knowledge of all things in nature, and better teaches to distinguish between truths and such things as have the appearance of being truths, yet are not, than any other. Their education, and the proper cultivation of the sense which God has given them, are the objects on which my happiness most depends. To inspire them with a love of everything that is honourable and virtuous, though in rags, and with contempt for vanity in embroidery, is the way to make them the darlings of my heart. They should not only read, but it requires a careful selection of books; nor should they ever have access to two at the same time; but when a subject is begun, it should be finished before anything else is undertaken. How would it enlarge their minds if they could acquire a sufficient knowledge of mathematics and astronomy to give them an idea of the beauty and wonders of the creation! I am persuaded that the generality of people, and particularly fine ladies, only adore God because they are told it is proper, and the fashion to go to church; but I would have my girls gain such knowledge of the works of the creation, that they may have a fixed idea of the nature of that Being who could be the author of such a world. Whenever they have that, nothing on this side of the moon will give them much uneasiness of mind. I do not mean that they should be stoics, or want the common feelings for the sufferings that flesh is heir to; but they would then have a source of consolation for the worst that could happen.

Tell me how do the trees which I planted thrive? Is there shade under the three oaks for a comfortable summer-seat? Do the poplars grow at the walk, and does the wall of the terrace stand firm? My bankers tell me that all my money in their hands is exhausted by fees on the peerage, and that I am in their debt, which is a new epoch in my life, for it is the first time I was ever in debt since I was a midshipman. Here I got nothing; but then my expenses are nothing, and I do not want it particularly, now that I have got my knives, forks, tea-pot, and the things you were so kind as to send me.

EUGENE MARCEL PREVOST

The Chastity of Married Life

Even when couples remain, as people say, in love with each other, their love is of a peaceful and patient kind. This unexpected thing happens, which one would not believe if one had not experienced it – the presence of the accustomed companion at one's side becomes in the end an element of physical calm. Husbands do not, as a rule, care to confess it, and the wives who complain of being deserted are rare – most of us would find a renewal of our husbands' advances rather disagreeable. But nothing is more chaste, in reality, than the majority of households; nothing in them evokes passion. Passion depends upon uncertainty and brevity in regard to time; while the hours of a married couple are inordinately long and regular.

WILLIAM SHAKESPEARE

Sonnet 116

Let me not to the marriage of true minds
  Admit impediments. Love is not love
Which alters when it alteration finds,
  Or bends with the remover to remove.
O, no! it is an ever-fixed mark,
  That looks on tempests and is never shaken;
It is the star to every wandering bark,
  Whose worth's unknown, although his height be taken.
Love's not Time's fool though rosy lips and cheeks
  Within his bending sickle's compass come;
Love alters not with his brief hours and weeks,
  But bears it out even to the edge of doom.
  If this be error, and upon me proved,
  I never writ, nor no man ever loved.

ACKNOWLEDGEMENTS

The editor and publishers wish to thank the following for permission to use copyright material:

Carcanet Press Ltd for extracts from Robert Graves, *The Story of Mary Powell: Wife to Mr Milton*, Penguin (1954); and Helen Thomas, *World Without End* (1931), reissued as *Under Storm's Wing*;

Rosica Colin Ltd on behalf of the Estate of the author for an extract from Richard Aldington, *Death of a Hero*, Chatto & Windus (1929). © Estate of Richard Aldington;

Curtis Brown on behalf of the Estate of the author for extracts from Pamela Hansford Johnson, *The Humbler Creation* (1959). © 1959 Pamela Hansford Johnson;

Faber & Faber Ltd for an extract from C. S. Lewis, *A Grief Observed* (1961);

HarperCollins Publishers for extracts from Rosalind K. Marshall, *The Days of Duchess Anne*, Collins (1973);

The Harvill Press for lines by Julius Fucik, © Julius Fucik, taken from Reinhard Kuhn, ed., *Dying We Live*, (1956);

Macmillan General Books for extracts from Tamasin Day Lewis, *Last Letters Home*, (1995);

Penguin UK for Cecil Woodham Smith, *Life of Queen Victoria*, Hamish Hamilton;

CHILDHOOD · FRIENDSHIP · FIRST